Maid in West Ham

Maid in West Ham

My formative years, 1924–48

Ivy Alexander

ISBN: 978-0-9541545-0-9

© Copyright 2001 by Ivy Alexander

First Published in 2001 by:
Ivy Alexander
4A Fordington Road,
Winchester
Hampshire
SO22 5AL

Reprinted 2002
Reprinted 2004
Reprinted 2010

Cover designed by Christine Cox

Typset by PDQ Typesetting, Newcastle-under-Lyme.

Printed in Great Britain by The Baskerville Press,
Salisbury, Wiltshire.

Contents

	Introduction	vii
1.	My Parents' Forebears	1
2.	Early Years in Old Canning Town	14
3.	Secondary School Years and the Outbreak of War	36
4.	The Blitz and Farewell to Wharf Street	54
5.	The TB Clinic	70
6.	Adolescence in War-time West Ham	80
7.	Moving On: War Ends, and I Leave the Clinic	95
8.	Three Mills School, Stratford	108
9.	Fagin's Kitchen - A Happy Interlude	125
10.	A Trip to Post-war France	136
11.	Epilogue	146
	Appendix - Eric's account of 7th September 1940	155

Introduction

One of the earliest memories of my father is of seeing him writing in a large, thick, foolscap-sized ledger book. It was always a painful experience for us. We were a large family; the living room was small and we had only one table in the house. We interrupted his thoughts at our peril. Sometimes he would call in the young man from next door, George, to write at his dictation. My father apparently had a colourful past. I thought he had been famous. He had press cuttings and hand bills to prove it. These had to be preserved, almost worshipped. A framed photo, which was proudly displayed, stated that he was, 'Jimmy Hicks of Forest Gate. Ex-Bantam-weight Champion.' What was an 'Ex', I thought? I now know, sadly, that for my father, his life was virtually all 'Ex'. His brief claim to fame was in the past. The 'book' was kept in a wooden box, under his bed.

Without realizing its significance, and knowing nothing about genes, I, too, collected newspaper cuttings, programmes, letters and various memorabilia. These, like my father's, miraculously survived the blitz. After our house was destroyed in March 1941, I thought I had better bring them all together. So I went out and bought a large, thick, foolscap-sized ledger book, just like my father's. I went through my mother's biscuit tin full of photos, selected some negatives, had some printed, and began, 'Me. — By Ivy Hicks.' I kept this going for about ten years.

I did not have a colourful past to record. I was not an 'Ex', but I now realize that the period my book covers, which features the pre-war East End of London, the war years, evacuation, working in a TB clinic, teaching post-war culturally deprived children, and the awakening political consciousness of the 1940s, spans a significant period of the past.

When I married in 1951, I put the book away, not under the bed, but in the bottom of the wardrobe, which my father might have done, if he'd had a wardrobe. My son unearthed it many years later. He was fascinated and insisted that I do something with it. I put off the idea for some time, but as I have become aware that I am not immortal, I am now in a hurry to bring together what information I can find out about my past, to leave to my children. I have done this with the help of my 'diary', census returns, genealogical research, army and Local Government records, and reminiscing with friends and family, and relations.

My family, in particular, have been a great help and given me much encouragement, as have friends who read an earlier draft and suggested it might interest a wider audience.

Ivy Alexander
December 2000

Acknowledgements

I should like to thank my two sons, Peter and John, my daughter Clare, and my husband John for their encouragement and support.

In particular, I thank my husband John for his patience and forbearance. He has been closely involved in the production of the book throughout its entire gestation. Together we have walked the battlefields of the Somme and of Tunisia, the 'sewer bank' of West Ham and the waste lands of Old Canning Town. All these and other visits have helped me deepen my understanding of my memories and, I hope, make more sense of my recording of them. John read the proofs with interest, sensitivity and enjoyment, and this gave me the confidence to see the project through.

*For my family,
past, present and future.*

– 1 –

My Parents' Forebears

I was born Ivy Joan Hicks in the East End of London on the 17th September 1924; to be precise, in Wharf Street, Canning Town. I was one of a family of six, the progeny of James and Beatrice Hicks, unhappily joined in marriage. T. S. Eliot wrote, 'Home is where one starts from'. Yes... but perhaps one starts before even that. In later years I have tried to explore the gene pool from which I emerged. I turn now to some of the more significant drops in that pool.

'Change the name and not the letter, change for worse and not for better,' was an aphorism I was often to hear from my mother, as she wept into the tea towel hanging on the back of the kitchen door. She was born a Homes and married a Hicks. I am sure her grief was based on something more fundamental than an initial letter. But her mother's maiden name was Hawkins, and she married a Homes. For whatever reason that marriage was not to last. However, not till grandmother had borne five children, did she leave my grandfather 'a saint of a man', according to my mother. My sister, a Hicks, fell in love with a Hughes. Oh dear! She was not superstitious, but nevertheless, marriage was followed by divorce. I had a brief friendship with a Richard Hadfield, witty, intelligent, sensitive, good-looking and with wealthy parents. But that 'H'! I finally settled for an 'A'. Could my mother have avoided her mis-match, I wonder?

As a child I knew very little of my parents' background. My mother was more communicative than my father and I am grateful for those occasional glimpses she gave us of her early years. My father was a professional boxer and kept many mementoes of his early boxing days, and these were helpful. Over the years I have come to fill in many of the gaps in my knowledge and have more understanding now of how my parents were 'shaped'. Their marriage, and my upbringing, in turn helped to shape me. No doubt I in turn, together with my husband John, have had some influence on our children. And so on ad infinitum.

I always thought my parents were an ill-matched couple, and wondered how it came about that they were living together. In my early years they were the only role model I had of two people living together, sharing a bed and raising a family, yet I was not conscious of any warmth or loving relationship between them. Apart from the everyday minutiae of domestic

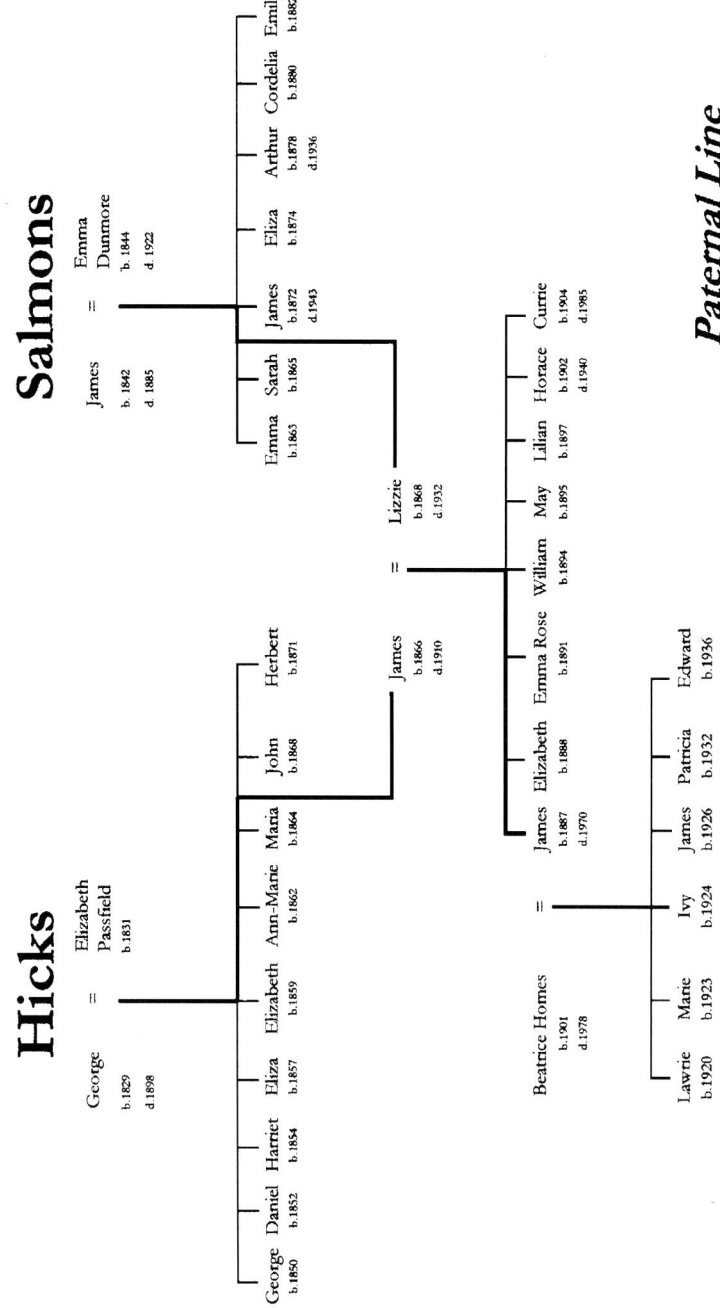

MY PARENTS' FOREBEARS

Emma Salmons, nee Dunmore. b.1844. d.1922.
With two of her six daughters.
Father's grandmother

My father, b.1887. d.1970.
With his first wife, Charlotte

affairs, they had no shared interests. I remember no meaningful or interesting discussions or conversations between them and I was aware that if my mother could have 'escaped', she would have done so. It was in this tense environment that six children were born and it is not surprising, therefore, that living as we did in a two up and two down house, with no bathroom, there was constant friction. How did two so very incompatible people meet and marry?

What I do know, is that my mother married in haste, in 1920, when she was eighteen years old, to get away from home and to spite her mother, it would seem. My father, too, seems to have married in haste, and not with a shot-gun in his back, either. Perhaps he married my mother before she had a chance to change her mind. I recently discovered that he was already married. Although his first wife, Charlotte, had petitioned for divorce on the grounds of physical cruelty, the decree was not yet absolute. It came nine months later. Oh, dear!

My father was born in 1887 and his forebears were mostly agricultural labourers from Essex, although I did discover an apprentice shoemaker (Census, 1841) and a blacksmith. In 1871, his grandfather, George Hicks, an agricultural labourer, was living in Ilford, with his market gardener wife, and eight of their ten children. So not only was his grandmother able to supply her large family with fruit and vegetables, but her produce must have been in great demand, as the neighbouring towns were rapidly expanding. However by 1881, he had become a labourer on the brick-fields at Wanstead Flats. As a child, I associated Wanstead Flats with happy days out. During the school holidays, it was a great treat to be taken there, or to Wanstead Park. With a picnic and a relaxed atmosphere, they were days to remember. It was a different picture in 1881. My father's grandfather would not have become a labourer on the brick-fields by choice. He had suffered the fate of many other agricultural labourers in the 1870's who were forced to seek work in the towns. With the introduction of agricultural machinery and increased imports, the demand for farm labourers declined. Illiterate and uneducated, and owning nothing, they were the perfect fodder for an expanding industrial society. Bricks were in great demand, and so for the Hicks family, a bothy on the brick-field replaced the cottage, and bricks not brassicas were produced.

It was here that my father's father spent his teenage years, and where he met Lizzie, a fellow brickmaker's daughter. They were soon married in the parish church of Wanstead. Three months later, my father was born. He was named James, after his father, and also after Lizzie's father. Lizzie was still living with her mother, Emma Salmons, who was running a laundry on the Flats, to support six of her eight children. Her husband had died two years previously, aged 43 years. According to a coroner's report, he had 'acciden-

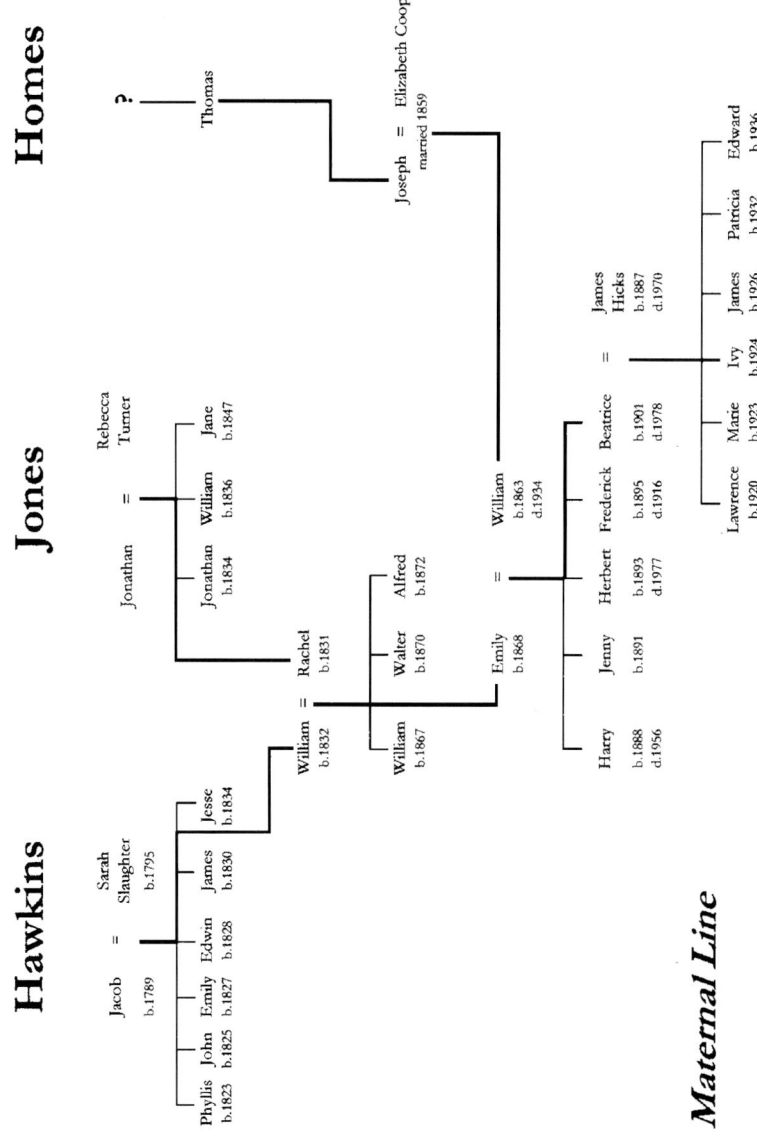

William Hawkins, b.1832

Rachel Hawkins, neé Jones, b.1831, d.1912

Emily Homes, neé Hawkins, b.1868, d. 1953

Mother Beatrice, aged 16 yrs. With her father, William.
Beatrice, b.1901, d.1978
William Homes, b.1863, d.1934

tally fallen from a cart'. My father was born at the laundry. Incidentally, like Lizzie's father, my father's father also died aged 43 years, but from a heart condition. However, by the time they had met their fate, both had bequeathed to posterity a generous supply of genetic material. According to my father, his mother went on to have twenty one pregnancies, but what with miscarriages and still births, I know of only eight who survived to maturity.

I had very little contact with my father's brothers and sisters, and he certainly had no photos to show us. This was probably due to the fact that he left home at the age of ten years, so he was not there when most of them were born. There used to be an annual fair on Wanstead Flats and a regular feature was the boxing booth. Four or five young lads would be invited into the ring at the same time to fight each other and the last one left standing was the winner. I believe he was given a coconut. My father got involved in all this and was often used by the proprietor to help gather a crowd. When the fair moved off, my father went too, and travelled around with it for many years. With his mother being fully occupied with pregnancy and childbirth, and house room being at a premium, I don't suppose many tears were shed for his absence. When the sporting newspaper *The Mirror of Life* organized a contest for the Bantamweight championship of England in 1906, my father was the winner. Although when in his prime he was reported to have won fifty contests by knockout blows, he himself took severe punishment. He had an estimated five hundred contests, and he too was occasionally knocked out and couldn't always remember the fight he'd had the previous night. When he eventually returned home, his brothers and sisters didn't know who he was.

He returned to Forest Gate to live. It sounds such an attractive place 'the gate to the forest', – Epping Forest. So it may have been at one time, but in reality it had become part of West Ham, a rapidly expanding town, which had grown without due regard to proper roads or drainage. Forest Gate was then regarded as the better part of West Ham, and at the height of my father's career, he continued to live there. He was well known, and to his satisfaction, at least, he had become 'somebody'. As a young man, well travelled, and with a bob or two in his pocket, he was attractive to women. At the age of nineteen, in 1906, he met and married Charlotte Bocater and they had three surviving children. They did not live in domestic bliss. Quite the contrary in fact, and Charlotte petitioned for divorce fourteen years later. What a pity she did not have a word in my mother's ear. But would she have listened, I wonder?

My mother, Beatrice Homes, was born in Poplar, East London in 1901. Her father's forebears had been Londoners for generations and seem to have been artisans. Census returns show a hatter, card maker, stone pol-

 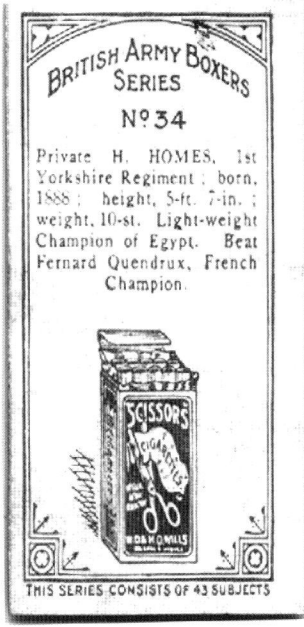

Wills cigarette card from 1913 featuring Harry Homes.

Frederick Homes, b.1895, d.1916. *Jenny, b.1891.*

isher and saw cutter. Her father was a chef. Her mother's family, the Hawkins, came from south of the Thames. Three generations back they were in Billinghurst, West Sussex, and like most people at that time, had occupations associated with the land. Jacob Hawkins in 1789 was a bailiff on a large farm, overseeing several labourers. His son William married the daughter of a watchmaker. My mother was always proud to relate that her great grandfather 'had made clocks for the Great Exhibition in 1851'. He was in fact a watch-maker.

However, as the agricultural depression of the late nineteenth century progressed, whilst my father's forebears moved south towards the great metropolis in search of work, my mother's forebears were moving north to achieve the same goal. Grandmother Emily Hawkins was born in 1868 in Penge, then in Surrey, but now part of south east London. I don't know how she came to meet William Homes, my grandfather, who was living in Bethnal Green, but they married at Christ Church, Shoreditch, in 1888. Mother, the fifth child, was born in 1901 in Dee Street, Poplar, just across the border from West Ham, where my father was born. But their fate was yet to be sealed. At this time, 1901, father was fourteen, still travelling with a fair, boxing for a living, and having some success at it.

When mother was eight years old, her mother left the family home, to live with a licensed victualler, with whom she ran various public houses for over thirty years, until his death in 1940. Grandfather William Homes was left to care for the family. He worked as a Chef at the Mansion House in London, and was able to bring home food. My cousin recalls a giant bread pudding, baked in a large, catering-sized dish, which would last for a week. The eldest child, Harry, born in 1888, was no longer at home, having been in the Army, the 1st Yorkshire Regiment, for some time. He, too, was a successful boxer, and in fact was the Army Lightweight Champion of Egypt in 1913. He had the distinction of appearing in a set of Wills cigarette cards, brand 'Scissors', in a series on British Army Boxers. I had some difficulty tracking down this card. With the passage of years the details had been lost. I did not know the name of the cigarette company, the series, the date or the country in which his boxing prowess had been displayed. I began to think it was perhaps just family folklore. Eventually a specialist in boxing memorabilia was able to locate the card, which I now proudly possess. It is nearly ninety years old. The next child, Jenny, was also no longer at home, being happily married. She actually emigrated to New Zealand in 1923. The third child, Bert, was then sixteen. He later played football for Tranmere Rovers.

But mother's favourite, and the brother closest to her, was Frederick, the fourth child, then aged thirteen. He and my mother, reputedly, 'ran the house'. All was well, until, in 1914, when mother was thirteen, Bert married and set his wife up in the family home, in Benares Road, Plumstead, south east London. My mother's position was usurped, and Bert's wife, Lala, soon took over. When two children quickly followed, according to my mother, she became Lala's 'skivvy'. The home was no longer a place to which she felt happy to invite friends. However, young Bert, Lala's first born, has happy memories of these times. He has filled me in with many aspects of my mother's early years. He said he was devoted to her.

Whilst Fred was still there, my mother found the situation bearable, but the outbreak of war, and conscription in January 1916, was to change things. Fred, being single, and just twenty one, was snapped up. He enlisted at Woolwich and was placed in the newly formed 16th Battalion of the Rifle Brigade. He was a gentle man, and had no desire to use a rifle to shoot anybody. However, the battalion was sent to France in March 1916. Although my mother heard no more, she was always hopeful he would return and when Armistice Day arrived and she had heard nothing, she was even more optimistic. And then the 'bomb-shell' came. He was missing, presumed killed. We always understood that Uncle Fred was killed on Armistice Day. 'Just imagine!' said my mother. 'Another day and he would have been saved. He was killed by a stray bullet. Mercifully it was quick.' On the 11th November, every year. mother would shed a tear. 'He was a lovely man. Kind and gentle. The only man I ever really loved'.

It took me some time to discover the circumstances of his death, as I firmly believed he had died on the 11th November 1918. With the help of the Rifle Brigade records, held at the Peninsular Barracks, Winchester, another story unfolded. He was actually killed at the Battle of the Somme, on the 7th October 1916. Records show that the battalion was in action around a tributary of the Somme, the river Ancre, which flows through Albert. On the 5th October the men were in the trenches, and Fred was in the front line. An account of that time reads, 'In October the weather worsened and the Somme became an impassable sea of mud'. Fred was not killed cleanly by a stray bullet as my mother believed, but had slithered and squelched in mud-filled trenches and then either been blown to pieces or wounded and left to die in the mud. His name appears on a memorial at Thiepval, together with over 73,000 others with 'no known graves', and no recovered bodies. 90% of these were killed between July and November, 1916. It was just as well the facts of her favourite brother's death were never known to my mother. His name also appears in a book of remembrance on display in Winchester Cathedral, dedicated to the 11,575 members of the Rifle Brigade who lost their lives in the 1914 to 1918 war. I have seen both this and his name on the memorial at Thiepval.

Fred was killed, touchingly, the same day as the poet Sergeant Leslie Coulson, nearby. After his death, a poem by Coulson was found, entitled,

Thiepval memorial

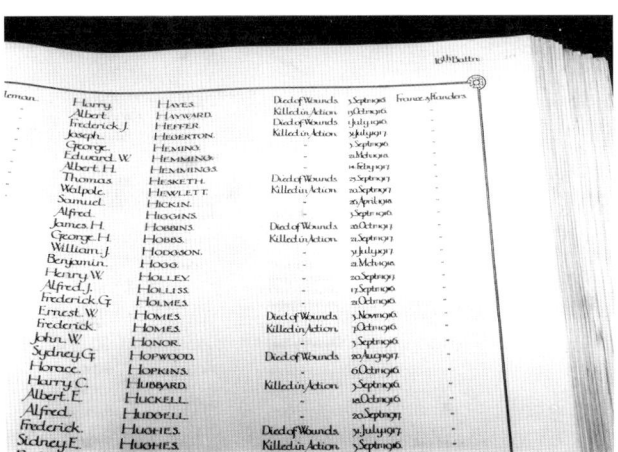

Memorial book, Winchester cathedral

'Who made the Law?' It begins:

> Who made the Law that men should die in meadows?
> Who spoke the word that blood should splash in lanes?
> Who gave it forth that gardens should be bone-yards?
> Who spread the hills with flesh, and blood, and brains?
> Who made the Law?

Rest in peace, Uncle Fred. Knowing Fred would not be returning and being unhappy at home, my mother left. Her father was most unhappy to see her go. With Fred being killed at the Somme, his favourite daughter's departure was a double blow. My mother and her father had a warm, loving relationship. He never raised his voice in anger and apparently, 'Beatrice could do no wrong'. Young cousin Bert, too, was upset. For many years afterwards, he was taken to visit my mother. But now, with mother and Fred gone, Bert and Lala had the house to themselves.

At this time, my mother's mother, Emily, was living in Wharf Street, Canning Town, in West Ham, on the other side of Bow Creek from Dee Street, where my mother was born. It was here that my mother went, expecting a warm reception no doubt. It was shortly afterwards that she met my father. He was well known in West Ham and she had heard of him through her brother Harry, as both were known in boxing circles. According to my brother Lawrie, who has my father's book of memoirs and cuttings, my father, Jimmy Hicks, was organizing a charity boxing show at East Ham Town Hall and he employed my mother as his cashier. She was eighteen and naïve and soon became the object of his desire, notwithstanding that he was already married and with three children. However, his wife Charlotte had recently petitioned for divorce, so no doubt he felt free to pursue the young Beatrice Homes. When the relationship developed, her mother objected. I knew my grandmother. She was a very positive and forceful woman and always spoke her mind. Being unable, or unwilling, to return to her father and having incurred her mother's wrath, young Beatrice was trapped. Against all advice she went to Southampton with 'Jimmy Hicks, of Forest Gate', who was by then a boxing promoter. She stayed in a hotel and he stayed in Derby Road. They were soon married by special licence on 7th February 1920. Not having parental permission, she stated at the Registrar's Office that she was twenty two years old and that her parents were dead. My father was recorded as being thirty one and a bachelor. In fact he was thirty three and the divorce from Charlotte was not made final and absolute until the 1st November. Obviously very little checks were made at the Registrar's office. I have only recently discovered this information for myself. It is of no consequence now, as all those concerned are no longer with us, so may 'sleeping dogs lie'.

Up to that time, my mother had never slept with anybody, not even a sister, unlike myself who slept first with one and then with two. 'I didn't know what to expect,' she said. She was soon to find out.

They returned to rooms in Forest Gate. Ten months later when my brother Lawrie was born, my mother had no idea how he would be delivered. She thought she would have to be slit open. The marriage caused a rift between mother and daughter, which was to last for ten years. Grandmother must have been of some help, however, because shortly after Lawrie was born, she left Wharf Street and my parents were able to rent the property. The next five children, including myself, were born there.

But we are shaped by more than our genes. Growing up in Old Canning Town also had a lasting impact on me.

– 2 –

Early Years in Old Canning Town

I was the third child, born in 1924. My arrival was not awaited with any great joy, my elder sister Marie having been born only 17 months previously. When she was born, in the upstairs bedroom, people in the street below were rejoicing. This was not to celebrate her birth. They were singing, 'I'm forever blowing bubbles...'. There were cries of, 'We've won! We're in the final!' West Ham had done well that day.

Except for my eldest brother, we were all born at home, in Wharf Street, a two-bedroomed, terraced house in that part of West Ham known as Old Canning Town. I used to think that the area was called 'old' because it was shabby and 'well-worn', but now understand it was 'old' in historical terms. Canning Town began to emerge in the middle of the nineteenth century, at the northern end of Plaistow marshes and close to a ship-yard, which later became the Thames Ironworks and Shipbuilding Company. Incidentally, it was the Thames Ironworks Football Club which in 1900 became West Ham United. Development was confined to the area between the River Lea on the West and the Eastern Counties Railway branch line to the east. Earlier roads may have gone right up to the River Lea, but by the time I was born, these had been replaced by wharves and gas-works. Roads had been truncated, which explains why the area to the west of Bidder Street, which ran north to south, was a mystery to me. Fragments of roads led to gates and factories and I was certainly unaware that a river lay beyond. Old Canning Town was the narrow strip of land, wedged between the wharves and the gas-works on the west, and the railway, with Stephenson Street running alongside, to the east. It had the appearance and feeling of an area left over by accident. It was best left to atrophy. Its earlier reputation as an area where one would not venture alone, for fear of 'footpads', had lingered, as had many memories of the past. Older folk still spoke of the Iron Bridge and the Marshes. When we went out to play, we were instructed not to go 'over the Iron Bridge' or 'down the Marsh'. The Iron Bridge, across the River Lea, had long since been replaced as a crossing by a new road linking East India Dock Road to Barking Road. 'Down the marsh' referred to Victoria Dock Road, which to me, as a child, seemed a foreign place anyway, frequented by 'blackmen' who wore their shirts outside their trousers. These were the Lascars. Some of their families lived in

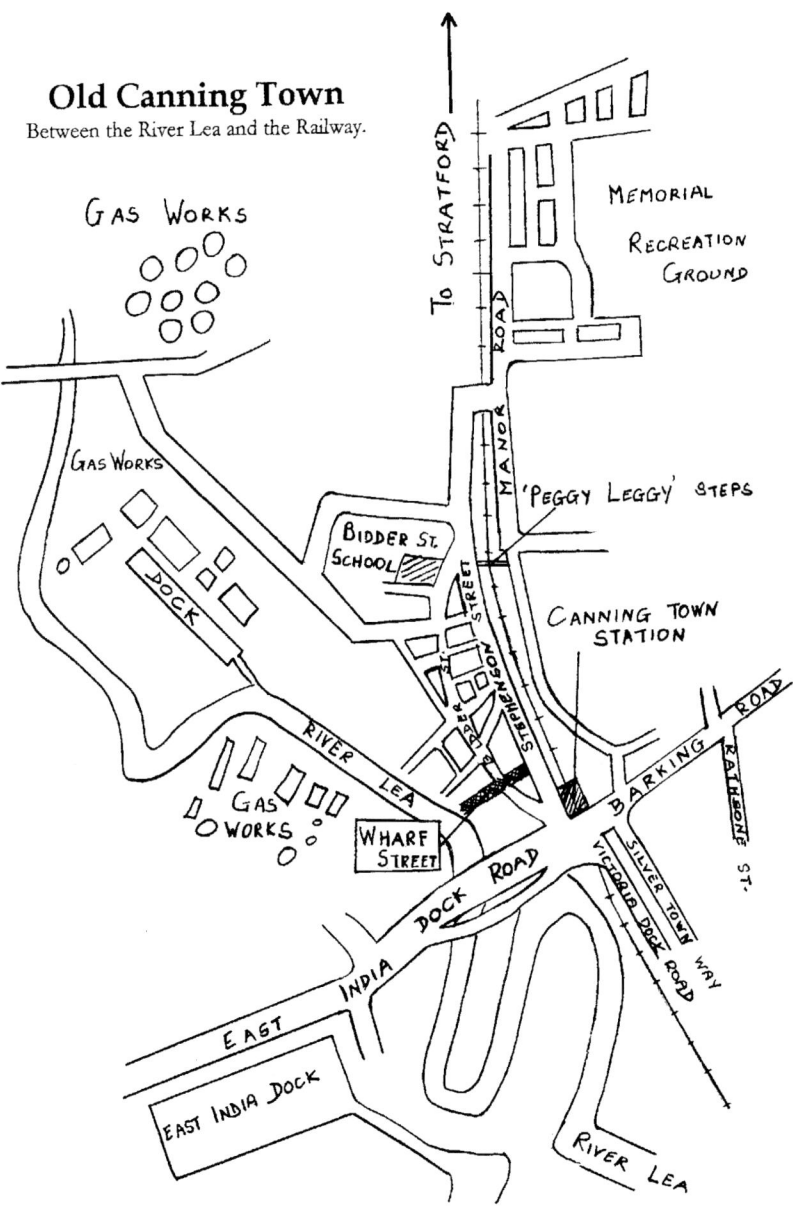

and around Victoria Dock Road and they lived wretched lives.

In this ellipse, or rather elongated 'D'-shaped area of a quarter of a mile or less, lived a human population of several thousand. It contained a school in Bidder Street which was built in 1877 for 750 pupils and a delightful church, St. Gabriel's, with a vicarage set in its own grounds. There were more than a dozen streets, some of them, like Wharf, Lea, Creek, Ship and Shipwright reflecting their dock-side proximity. Stephenson Street and Bidder Street, of course, were after the great railway engineers and were no fitting monument to their memory. Bidder also designed the Victoria Docks. I do not know who Randal Street was named after, but I know it contained an evil-smelling flock factory, and the fragments of shredded rags blew about everywhere. Here also was the Paragon bleach works. The names Quadrant Street and Junction Street are self-explanatory, and Wellington Street was obviously after the Duke. Before my time there used to be a public house of that name there. When I knew it, it was a community centre, run by 'missionary' workers from one of the universities. It housed a very popular nursery school, which my brother attended and the Towns Women's Guild, of which for a time my mother was chairman. There was also a 'club' night which I enjoyed. In Quadrant Street there was a medical 'mission' which served a very useful purpose as there were no GPs in the area, even if we could afford one. Ghandi paid a visit there in the early thirties, but I can find no reference to this anywhere, or to the Wellington community centre.

In the triangle enclosed by the streets Ship, Bidder and Junction, were the Alleys. This was a very congested area, with scores of tightly packed houses, each no larger than a shack in a South African township and just as deprived. It was a 'no-go' area in a 'no-go' district. When I was eight years old, I ventured there once, and was chased by a gang of boys, and I ran for my life, or so I thought. My sister, just a year older than me, turned round to fight them off, and they fled. This was the first area to be demolished under the slum clearance scheme in the thirties. No other houses replaced them so we had an additional play area. All the roads, except one, were named 'streets'. There were no Avenues, Crescents, or Drives. These were the addresses of 'posh' people. The one exception was New Road, the most northerly road, and probably the last to be built.

Most families were large and houses were small. The streets were narrow, but as nobody had cars they became our play areas. When I stood in Wharf Street recently, a couple of lorries occupied the space where nine houses had been, five on one side of the road and four opposite, these wedged between a sack factory and Wood's paint factory. In those nine houses, just before the Second World War, lived sixty people. There were hundreds of families in Old Canning Town, and these were served by a

EARLY YEARS IN OLD CANNING TOWN

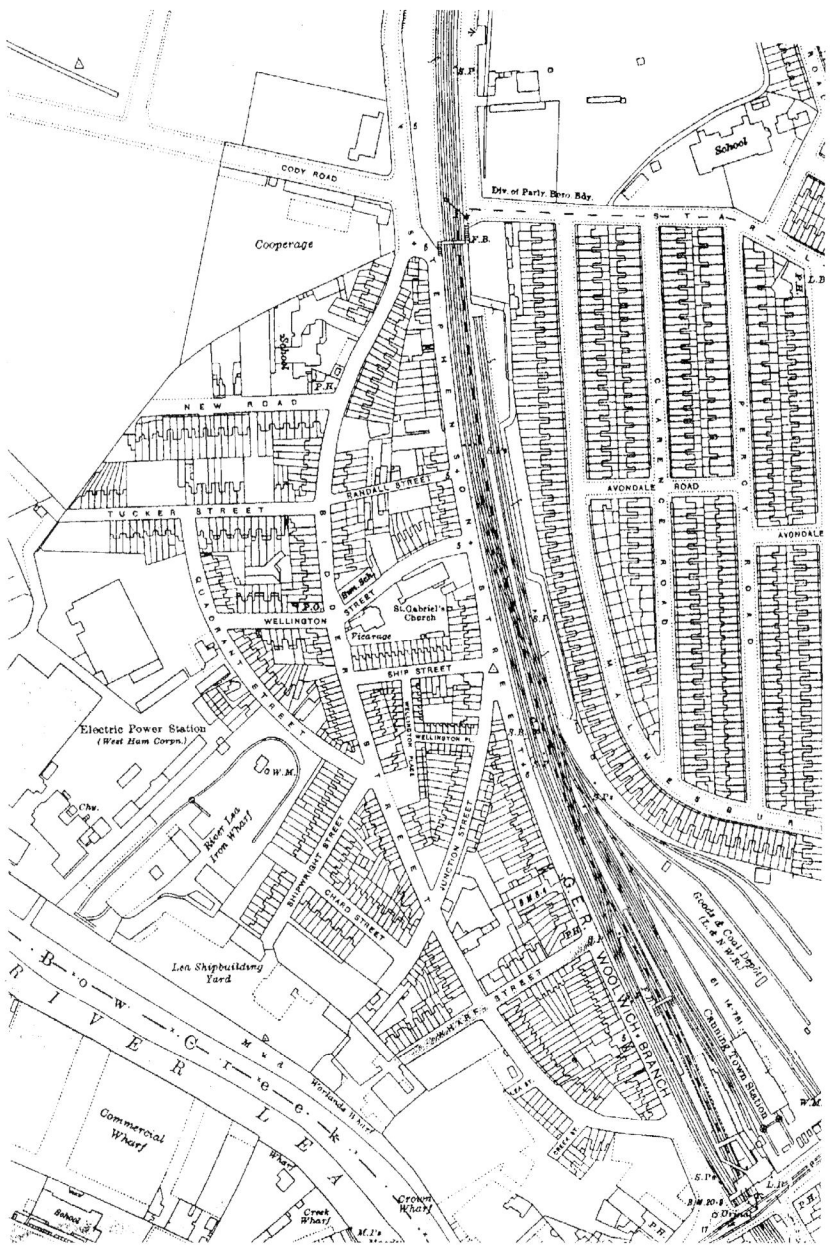

Old Canning Town – 1916 – between the LNER and the River Lea.

great variety of shops. In Bidder Street there were several general stores, a green-grocer's, a barber's, butcher's and fish and chip shop. There was a hard-ware shop, a veritable Aladdin's cave, where we could buy paraffin, candles, mouse-traps, sticky fly-catchers, canes for our chastisement and Sunlight soap. Close by was a 'cook shop' where one could buy a take-away dinner or soup provided you took your own plate, basin or jug. On the way to school there were two sweet-shops. With two pubs, including the Durham Arms at the corner of Wharf Street and Stephenson Street, Old Canning Town was very well served. Everything was available. It was a self-contained community. All it lacked was an undertaker's and a cemetery, and for many people access to these facilities was the only way out.

The type of housing in the area has been well documented, and 6, Wharf Street, where I lived, was no exception. The houses fronted directly on to the pavement. Each had a wooden window 'shutter' fixed to the wall. Our pride and joy was a strip of garden at the back. Beyond our garden and in somebody else's back, was a large mature tree, a survivor of West Ham's rural past. The road itself was divided by Bidder Street, with the wharf gates at one end and Stephenson Street at the other. In our section, on the opposite side of the road to us, on the corner of Bidder Street, was what had been a large substantial house with an imposing frontage surrounded by railings. It was now dilapidated and formed part of a sack factory. The women workers there were the most depressed I have ever come across. They had sacks covering their heads and shoulders, folded to provide a hood, but they were still covered from head to toe in a fine dust, which smelt of pepper. There was a terrace of four houses opposite to us. There used to be six, but two were demolished to make way for a paint factory. This was close to, and over-looking our front rooms. The large sliding gate was set back slightly from the wall, and the alcove thus formed made a cosy nook for courting couples on dark nights, after leaving the adjacent Durham Arms, no doubt. This provided a good source of entertainment for my sister Marie and I. Night after night, when we should have been tucked away safely, we peered through our bedroom window and discovered the facts of life.

Number six Wharf Street was in a terrace of five houses. It had two small bedrooms and two small rooms downstairs and a single-storied back scullery with a sloping roof and a concrete floor. The front room downstairs was called 'the parlour'. It contained a piano and a three-piece suite, with a wooden plant stand and an aspidistra in the window. It was only used on Christmas Day and Boxing Day when the fire was lit and we roasted chestnuts. It was always kept tidy, 'in case anybody comes', but it was far too cold to be inviting. The outside toilet, which was built on to the scullery, was flushed by 'pulling the chain'. The cistern was attached to the wall, high up and beyond our reach. The seat was a wall-to-wall wooden plank with a hole in it. Nailed to the wall was a sheaf of neatly torn up newspaper. Replenishing the stock was a task my father took upon himself. Newsprint was a common source of toilet paper in those days, but we liked to think ours was better organized than most. The scullery contained a copper, which was heated by solid fuel at the base, a single tap, an earthenware sink, and later a gas cooker. It led off the living room, which we called the kitchen. It had in it a 'kitchener' stove, fired by coal and used for heating and cooking. It was kept burning for most of the year and always had a kettle of water steaming on it. It was surrounded by a fire-guard and a steel fender with the words 'Home Sweet Home' built into the design. On the floor was a rug, which my mother made by hooking strips of rag on to sacking. My sister and I spent far too much of our childhood polishing the stove with 'zebo' and the fender with emery paper.

The kitchener stove and the fire-guard I well remember. One winter's evening, when my parents were out, and the temperature was well below zero, my brother Lawrie explained how water could be turned into ice and placed an enamel cup of water on the outside window ledge. After it froze, he said he could turn it back into water again and placed the cup on the very hot stove. I was four years old at the time and was fascinated. In my eagerness to watch the experiment I leant over the fire-guard to witness the transformation. I tilted forward and fell on to the stove, left cheek down. Lawrie pulled me off by the legs, and although my face was severely burned, his prompt action no doubt saved me from permanent disfigurement. Incidentally, brother Jimmy, who was then two years old, developed a squint about this time and it was firmly believed this was due to the shock he suffered on waking up and finding me next to him with my head swathed in bandages. The squint remained until he took himself off to Poplar Hospital at the age of seventeen to have it corrected.

Eventually six children were reared in this two-bedroomed house and, inadequate though it was, this type of housing was better than most in the area. Further into the 'old town' the quality of housing deteriorated. However, many of these were demolished in the early '30's under a slum clearance scheme for which we did not qualify, much to my mother's disappointment. A constant battle was waged to keep these houses clean and free from vermin. Bugs were in the brickwork and plaster, and difficult to eradicate. They got behind the wallpaper in the bedrooms. My mother stripped the wallpaper off and painted the walls, but bugs still got into the bed springs and in the folds at the end of the mattress. The beds were constantly being dismantled and painted with 'turps' to kill the bugs. We would squash them with our fingers on the walls, the result of which was not a pretty sight. Our friend Ethel next door but one had a better idea. She said if you held a lighted candle underneath the bugs, they would drop off, and then you could tread on them. We watched her from outside doing this one night, and had a good laugh. Ethel later worked as a domestic help at one of the houses where 'missionary' workers lived. She responded to helpful advice and blossomed in these improved living conditions. She changed her name to Eve, and put her past behind her.

Although as neighbours we were on reasonably good terms, there was no practice of 'dropping in'. People's privacy was respected. We played in the narrow street outside our front doors. Strangers, or non-residents were easily recognised. These would usually be official callers, including, in our case, the insurance man from the Liverpool Victoria. As each child was born, he would gain another customer, the weekly contribution being one penny per week. A lump sum was paid on death, thus assuring a respectable funeral. My mother was never to receive any lump sum, fortunately, I suppose. There was also the rent collector, who came for his ten shillings and sixpence (52p) every week, the gas-meter man, who emptied the penny- in- the- slot meter, and the electricity meter reader. Sometimes there would be a caller from the Relief Office, the R.O. man. We were given strict instructions about strange callers. 'If anybody comes asking questions, you know nothing. Hear that? Nothing!' Strangers were definitely suspect.

We rarely entered neighbours' houses and never entered the bedrooms, so where everybody slept was a mystery. As for us, we had various arrangements with the addition of each child. Five children presented no problems. The children were in one bedroom and the parents in another. When the sixth child, Edward, was born, my parents slept on a bed-settee in the living room. We then had three boys in one bedroom and three girls in another. This arrangement was not entirely satisfactory. Whenever we had friends round, my father would open the bed-settee and start preparing for bed, to our great embarrassment.

The storing of our clothes was a problem, but was eased somewhat by the fact that there was a paucity of supply. We were fortunate if we had something to wear and something in the wash. We had no pyjamas and underclothing was communal. We wore what we were given. Choice did not enter into it. We had no personal drawer space. All clothes and household linen were kept on shelves in the back bedroom cupboard, and shoes kept in the kitchen cupboard under the dresser to the left of the fireplace. We just helped ourselves to what would fit. The storage situation took a turn for the better in 1932, when grandmother Lizzie died, aged 64. She was then living in Woodstock Road, Forest Gate, in rented property. I had no feeling of sadness, as we'd had very little contact. Her remaining offspring, six of them I believe, gathered together after the funeral and selected what furniture they wanted, taking it in turns in order of seniority. My father was first, so mother selected a large Victorian chest of drawers, which was put to very good use whilst we lived in Wharf Street. So far as I am aware, that was my father's entire legacy – and he had first choice! When my mother's father died in 1934, her brother Bert and family were living in the house, so there was no legacy there.

I don't know how Ethel's family managed for space with eight children. The houses opposite had three bedrooms but then Mrs. Crush had 9 children. Come to think of it, what an apposite name that was. Mrs. Bush next door had seven children, but sadly Mr. Bush lay dying in one of the bedrooms for years before succumbing to cancer. The other two houses had two families in each. Children, however, continued to be procreated, though considerable subterfuge had to be exercised. Sending the children to Sunday school was one solution. Ethel's father's plan was even more ingenious. Ethel was sent on a long journey, after Sunday lunch, together with younger brothers and sisters, to buy winkles and watercress for tea.

When we were younger we were not upset by our cramped conditions. We spent as little time as possible in the house. Except for bedtime, or when we were scrubbing and cleaning, or when we were at school, we were playing in the street and great fun we had too. We played rounders, using neighbours' window shutters for bases. We tied rope to a lamp-post and swung round it. There was whip and top, hopscotch, skipping and marbles in the gutter. One dark night we made toffee, and together with Ethel and a few other friends, we stuck all the door knockers down with it. We had plenty of friends and always had younger brothers and sisters to look after. The street was a good playground, unlike today. Nobody had cars and the roads were traffic free. The street was a communal meeting place. Mrs. Bush, opposite, had a daughter who suffered from cerebral palsy. Trixie was seated in her wooden, high-backed push-chair, outside her house, on the pavement, all day. Everybody passing by spoke to her, although what poor Trixie said was unintelligible. A young man, a fellow sufferer, in Bidder Street, had a similar experience.

In the summer people sat at the front of their houses and watched the children play, or just chatted. The houses round the corner from us, in Stephenson Street, had a small fenced area at the front, about five feet deep, which contained a bench. These were ideal meeting places, especially at Mrs. Brown's. Mrs. Brown's daughter, Lil, had a job putting fasteners at the end of pearl necklaces. She brought strings of these home from work by the gross and would sit for hours attaching the fasteners at lightning speed. Anybody leaving the 'Old town' had to pass through Bidder Street or Stephenson Street, so Mrs. Brown, sitting on her bench, knew most people and what was going on. People in trouble often went to Mrs. Brown, my mother included. One woman who regularly passed by, wore

Marie, Ivy and Lawrie. Summer 1926

*Back row: Grandfather, cousin Bert, and father
Front row: Marie, Ivy and Lawrie.
In garden at Wharf Street, 1926*

Marie, mum, Jimmy and Ivy. Summer 1928

Mother, with Patricia, born 1932.

the same suit for as long as I could remember, winter and summer. Whenever she passed, she remarked, 'It's a lovely day', or 'Isn't it cold today', followed by, 'You don't know what to wear do you'. Mrs. Brown helped everybody. When the river Lea overflowed, as it did on two occasions whilst I lived there, our house was flooded. On the first occasion, water gradually crept up the kitchener stove, hissing as it went. We were four children then, and I remember being carried over the back garden to Mrs. Brown's, whose house was at a slightly higher level than ours.

Women generally had a very hard time. They were trapped. Birth control was not considered. 'The men won't have it,' said my mother. It was not until just before the war that my mother and her two fertile neighbours began to talk about Marie Stopes, but not before Ethel's mother nearly bled to death after a self-induced abortion. I was not aware of any child sexual abuse, but there was certainly wife-abuse. They were always available. Very few people were able to change their circumstances. In all the sixteen years that I lived in Wharf Street, nobody escaped. They were not in a position to do so. In the twenties and thirties there was a great deal of unemployment, and those at work were poorly paid. Work in the docks was casual, but men had to turn up in the hope of being selected. The young man next door, who left school at fourteen years, like everybody else, used to come home sometimes, with sore, sticky feet, when he was unloading sugar. He said it got into your shoes. He didn't complain as he was paid extra – 'dirty money' it was called. With poor pay, and so much unemployment, people were caught in a poverty trap. Another child meant a bit more R.O. – money from the Relieving Office. Although relief was later administered by the Public Assistance Committee, they still called it R.O. From the men's point of view, there was no reason to stop having children – they had their value.

One might have imagined that out of these oppressive conditions, some radical thought would have arisen, but, so far as I am aware, this was not the case. I witnessed no unrest amongst the unemployed and poorly paid in Old Canning Town. They were apathetic and accepted their lot. Ill-health may have had something to do with it, and for generations they had been grateful for whatever crumbs came their way. My mother, a reasonably intelligent woman, thought government was best left in the hands of those who had money. 'They know what to do with it', she said. 'Look at us. If we could govern, we wouldn't be in this state.' My father was not a member of a political party, or a Trade Union, but was the proud possessor of a large certificate which was framed and hung in the passage-way. This proclaimed that he was a member of the 'Antediluvian Order of Buffaloes'. This was as far as his membership went. When I enquired what the Buffaloes were, my mother said, 'The poor man's Freemasons'. So I was none the wiser.

The educational provision locally left much to be desired. Classes were large, and, compared with my experience today, children seemed to be lethargic, no doubt through under-nourishment and ill-health. Most children had no good role-model, and limited aspirations. To work in Woolworth's was the dream of many girls. Very few children were expected to pass the 'scholarship' examination at eleven years and very few did so. Until the early thirties, they remained at the school until they were fourteen and then left and took whatever job was available. Canning Town Board school, serving as it did an impoverished district, suffered from frequent staff changes. Things improved slightly in 1932 when Pretoria Road Senior School was built, on the other side of the railway line, and pupils

Brother Lawrie's class at Bidder Street School, Canning Town 1927.

were transferred from the Bidder Street School at the age of eleven.

Except for my youngest brother, Eddie, who was only three years old in 1939, when the onset of war changed the whole pattern of things, we all went to the local school. It was surrounded by a high brick wall, with an iron gate, which was kept locked. At break times some mothers would poke sandwiches through the bars for their children. How I envied them. Some children came to school bare-footed and some were provided with free boots, and heavy things they were too. Free dinners and breakfasts were provided for the needy, and for a time that meant us. We had a long walk to the school building which provided the free meals. It was on the other side of the railway, which we crossed by going over 'Peggy-Leggy' steps. This crossing had always been thus described, but I haven't found anybody who really knows why. The dinners were not as good as our mother cooked and I could not eat them. Unless one returned an empty plate to the counter, however, there was no 'afters'. I remember feeling hungry for a time, being without dinner or afters. Some children were less fastidious than we were, so we would get them to eat our dinner, too. Winnie Bush from across the road would often help me out, otherwise I would surreptitiously throw the food underneath the table, and was rewarded with rice, sago pudding or spotted dick.

The school day was from nine in the morning till midday and then from two till four o'clock, so there was a long break at lunch time. If we had free meals, we didn't go home and had to spend the time in the playground. There were no washing facilities. One afternoon we had a needlework lesson and after hemming a strip of material for about an hour, it looked decidedly mucky. 'Your hands are disgusting,' said the teacher, who was new to the school. 'Haven't you been taught how to wash?' She made me feel as though I was the lowest form of vermin. I felt so ashamed that I burst into tears. When I explained that I hadn't been home so I was unable to wash, she was unrepentant. To this day I still remember how humiliated she made me feel.

My father was unable to undertake regular employment being unsteady on his legs, 'due to the boxing', it was said. He walked with a shuffling gait, and his speech was slurred – the typical 'punch-drunk' syndrome. Although we qualified for free meals, Marie and I were so unhappy that we were allowed to forego this concession. We were reasonably well fed and adequately clothed, due to my parents' resourcefulness. By devious means the R.O. money was supplemented. My father sold leather bootlaces, pearl buttons and linen buttons, press studs and matches, from a tray slung round his neck, outside the Boleyn Arms, Plaistow, on a Saturday and Sunday. Another money earner for a short period was the selling of 'Hicks' Foot Salts', actually common soda and Epsom salts, which he sold from a stall

Handbill advertising my father's miracle cure.

in Rathbone Street. The soda was purchased in a large sack and he and my mother put it into small packets. Leaflets were put through doors advertising this miracle cure. My mother also bought two second-hand 'fairy-cycles' and let them out for a penny an hour. She iced cakes and machined garments for a small charge. At one time, Marie and I took mint from the garden, and sold it in Rathbone Street, to the cry of, 'Penny a bunch of mint!' My younger brother, Jimmy, used to 'mind' people's cars whilst they sat drinking in the Bridge House Tavern, a public house close to the old Iron Bridge. This ensured them against vandalism. My mother bought second-hand clothes from the 'Old Gels' in Chrisp Street, Poplar. The 'Old Gels' (girls) were women who obtained clothes from the more affluent members of society and sold them to the less well off. The clothes were unpicked, the sections washed and then machined into 'new' clothes for us. Mother also mended our shoes and I still have the hobbing foot she used. She was a very talented woman. As well as playing the piano 'by ear', she did very fine crochet, painting, decorating, and woodwork. She was chairman of the local Towns Women's Guild, and on several occasions our garden won an award in the best garden competition.

Some children were more deprived than others and to improve their health were sent to the Fyfield Open Air school, near Chipping Ongar, in Essex. When they returned, they had put on weight, were well-mannered and subdued and spoke posh. Once a year we were all given the opportunity to have a day in the country when the entire Junior School was taken by train to Loughton, and Epping Forest. The locals, apparently, anticipated our arrival with fear and foreboding. Myth and mystery abound as to what actually took place, but there is mention of children gorging themselves on meat pies and buns and of contaminated areas being sprayed with disinfectant after we had left. This was considered to be the origin of the term, 'Lousy Loughton'. As one who was on the receiving end of these philanthropic endeavours, it might be of interest to put on record my memories of those days.

In the summer term there was talk of Loughton. We were blackmailed into good behaviour – running errands, saving our pennies and other inducements, otherwise the great day would be denied us. The day before we left, we had instructions on good behaviour. The night before, in our house at least, we were put in the zinc bath and scrubbed clean and our best clothes laid out. On the day itself we were given pocket money and went to school as usual. There we were given a cardboard disc on string, to hang around our necks, and threatened with dire consequences should it be lost. I can remember it bore the words 'Ragged School Union' and 'Shaftesbury'. We couldn't think what it had to do with us.

We were marched to Canning Town station in crocodile fashion, along the whole length of Bidder Street. We sang as we marched like soldiers on the move. 'It's a long way to Lousy Loughton' seemed a good song. Where was Tipperary, anyway? We were cheered the whole way. As we assembled on the platform people looked over the wall alongside Stephenson Street, which ran parallel with the railway line, and as the train moved out of the station, family and friends lining the street waved us off. Teachers warned us in vain of the dangers of hanging out of train windows.

We continued to sing, through Stratford station and beyond, until we arrived at Loughton station. We then walked to the 'big hall', which I now know to be the 'Shaftesbury Retreat'. We probably had lunch then, and ate whatever was offered to us before being let loose into Epping Forest. We did the usual childish things: chased each other, fell into the mud, and got lost. Getting lost was my greatest fear. One tree looked much like another. We were accustomed to using friends' houses as markers. At the end of the day we were all collected – I don't know how – and returned to the Retreat for roll-call and tea. An annual ritual was the buying of gifts with our pocket money for every member of the family not lucky enough to be at Loughton. We bought such things as whistles, various 'blowers', brooches, cuff-links, hair slides, balls, pencils and small ornaments for the mantelpiece. All were obtainable at the Retreat. It seemed a long day and the sun always shone. We all enjoyed ourselves and nobody ever forgot the experience. We were welcomed back and met at the station with smiling faces, or so it seemed.

I was not then aware of the efforts of our forefathers to save Epping Forest, but what I do remember is the reverence the older generation had for the Forest – a reverence beyond my understanding, and which they had acquired from their parents and grandparents. Since delving into family history and genealogy, I now realize that many of us who landed up on the dust-heaps of East London, and who were granted the privilege of entering the Forest for one day a year, actually had our roots in Epping Forest. We were squeezed out during the nineteenth century as it became increasingly difficult to survive by working on the land. Doubtless on those school excursions to Epping Forest we did leave our mark. There were no portaloos in those days. I'm glad we did; it was our forest too. What a pity the area was sprayed. Autumn leaves and winter frosts would soon have done a first-class recycling job.

The origin of the term 'Lousy Loughton' is now becoming lost with the passage of time. There may be a cautionary tale here about historical evidence. At a lecture on Essex villages I once attended at Wansfell College, in Theydon Bois, it was suggested that the name 'Lousy Loughton' was associated with the fact that local people had to disinfect the place after the visit of East End children. 'Has anybody here heard the term?' we were asked. 'I have,' I replied. 'I was one of those children!' The lecturer was astonished and asked if I would write about the experience for the local History Society newsletter. 'Or you could speak into a tape-recorder,' he suggested. I did write! We East Enders imagined that we had thought up the term. It sounded good; it was alliterative; it sang well; it rolled off the tongue easily and was more euphonic than just 'Loughton'. We placed quite a different meaning to it when we happily sang of Lousy Loughton in the thirties. If we had gone to Southend, we would probably have marched to 'Sunny Southend'.

Another opportunity to escape the grime and smoke of Old Canning Town occurred with the annual exodus to the hop fields in Kent. Some families went every year, but we only went once. The event was a bit of a 'closed shop'. The farmer would have a regular contact who kept a list. In September, a few days before the hops were ready for picking, the invitation would be received. In our case, a family on Mrs. Mott's list was unable to go so we filled the breech. It was about 1929. We were four children then, Lawrie, Marie, myself and Jimmy, who was in hospital at the time. All the equipment and bedding to sustain us for three to five weeks had to be taken. We all, about twenty of us, travelled with the laden tea-chests in a lorry. On arrival we were allotted a hut with a wall-to-wall slatted wooden bunk, which was to be our bed. Straw was collected from the oast house,

1929, hop picking Top left: mother. 3: Mrs Mott. 4, 5, 6: Ivy, Marie, Lawrie

which was put into an empty mattress cover and bolster case for our bedding. Each day we collected the vines and dragged them to our allotted canvas bin and then picked the hops off one by one. It was hard work for the adults, trying to make some money, but we children had great fun. The school authorities turned a blind eye to our absence from school, believing no doubt that the fresh air would be beneficial.

We all had a wonderful time and took home plenty of 'hopping apples', or 'oppinapples' as we called them, Bramleys, I think. Our ecstasy was to be short-lived, however. On the way home in the lorry, and before we actually arrived at the house, we saw our father. We had all been singing and were excited. Marie put her cupped hand to her mouth as if blowing a trumpet, and made a noise. When we were deposited outside our house with all the luggage, we were denied entry. My father was berserk and lashed out at any of us within reach. To my mother, he said, 'You've been away for weeks, and now you've taught the fucking kids to blow raspberries at me. Well, you can stay away.' A crowd of neighbours collected and this crowd attracted more people who wanted to know what was going on. As they shouted and hissed, my father got more hopping mad. He went inside for a while, and soon the upstairs window flew open and a bucket of water was thrown at the crowd. We all went round to Mrs. Brown's, who took us in. I don't know how it was all sorted out, but we returned after a few days. Either

Top row: Albert Brown, Lawrie, Horace Brown. Front: Lilly Brown with Jimmy on lap, Ivy, Marie, Lizzy B, Mum. Summer 1927.

my father was missing his pork chops, or Mr. Brown had a man-to-man talk with him. After all, with four adult children, Lizzie, Lil, Jenny and Horace, and two bedrooms, life couldn't have been easy for him whilst we were there.

These violent outbursts of temper and foul language of my father continued to be a permanent feature of my childhood. Although my father could sometimes be very caring, and occasionally took us on trips, mostly to Wanstead Park or the Flats, generally, we felt it was better to keep out of his way. We were always on a 'knife-edge'. His sudden outbursts were always accompanied by a volley of Anglo-Saxon expletives, which after a time failed to have any impact, as they were considered to be part of his normal vocabulary. He would explode for no apparent reason. My mother thought a new moon had some relevance. Our living room was very small and was crowded with just a table, four chairs and a settee. When my father read a newspaper he would open it at arms length. In this situation, we got close to him at our peril. If perchance we did approach and touched the newspaper, it would snap shut, like a gin trap. The back of his hand, usually his left, would fly out and catch you across the face. 'You silly fucking bastard. Look where you're fucking going'. Another powder keg was meal times. He expected to be fed like a fighting cock, or a hard-working navvie, a hang-over from the days when the whole family went short to supply the man of the house, the sole provider, to give him strength to go out to work 'to bring home the bacon'. The kitchen table was placed under the window, which faced on to the back garden, home to the dog, 'Fluffy', but whose resemblance to a ball of fluff now left much to the imagination. It was tethered to its kennel by a heavy chain, stout enough to secure an elephant, or an ocean liner. In summer the window of the living room was always left open. Picture the situation... Father at the kitchen table, bolt upright, knife and fork at the ready. His meal is placed in front of him. He takes a bite at the pork chop. He always had to have meat. 'What the fucking 'ell do you call this?' and out of the window it would fly, like a frisbee. Fluff would think it was Christmas and endeavour to reach the unexpected delicacy. The chain is too short, so she barks and howls. Out comes father, kicks the 'fucking dog', which tries to retreat to the kennel. He then kicks the kennel. If we've got any sense, we're out in the street by now. If the window is closed, the dinner goes up the wall. The dividing walls were thin and our next-door neighbours heard this clatter and commotion, and it was a source of great hilarity. 'What's your wall decoration this week?' George would often say. We soon learned to develop a sense of humour and were able to recognise the absurdity of the situation. His speech being slurred, 'due to the boxing', he spoke indistinctly, like a man without dentures. If we could not understand him, and said, 'What?'

he would say, 'Don't 'What?' me, you ignorant bastard. Where's your fucking manners? Learn to speak properly.'

We were sometimes chastised with a cane, which was kept hanging on a hook by the side of the fire-place. This was not uncommon in those days, in fact the local hardware shop kept a good supply. I was once sent to buy one, by my mother, in fact. Father also had a walking stick, which was another weapon. I remember the occasion when electricity was first installed in the mid thirties. When all was complete, mother and father left to go to the Imperial, the nearby cinema. I was so thrilled by this miraculous invention that I excitedly switched the light on and off a few times. Alas he had not gone far enough. He saw me, came back, and whacked me with his stick. 'You stupid bastard! You'll break all the fucking lights. Get upstairs to bed!' I climbed the stairs like a mountain goat, being struck as I ran where the stick could reach. On these occasions we children looked after each other and I'm sure sister Marie came to bed with me.

He did have a sense of humour, which was however usually to other people's detriment. One day mother had gone to Edie's, (Edith's,) who ran the local fish and chip shop. She had been gone longer than the allotted span. 'Where's your mother?' says he. 'She's round Edie's' say I. He says nothing, which I think is strange. I hear him rummaging about upstairs. He comes down with an armful of blankets. 'Here', he says. 'Take these round to your mother. Tell her if she's going to stop all night, she'll need these'. In all innocence, I did just that. Mother's friendly chit-chat was soon brought to an end and she flew home like the wind. We often had street performers on the corner of Wharf Street and Stephenson Street, outside the Durham Arms. Some poor man, desperate to make some money, was chewing and swallowing razor blades. I felt so sorry. I rushed home and said, 'There's a poor man eating razor blades for money'. 'Oh dear. Poor bastard!' said my father. 'Take him these', and he gave me a collection of old razor blades, rusty and coated with a mixture of soap and bristle. Again, I did just that. Was I a slow learner, or something, or still at the stage where I obeyed my father's orders? Incidentally, once a year, the clients from the Durham Arms hired a coach and had an outing. As the coach departed, a shower of coins was thrown into the road, and we children all scrambled to get what we could. I can only remember getting my fingers trodden on.

However, not all was doom and gloom in those early days. There were always friends to play with. We shared experiences and we all went to the same school. One particularly happy event was the celebration of the jubilee of King George the fifth, in 1935. The street party was a great occasion. Bunting was spread across the road, strung from one upstairs window to the one opposite. We swept the street, and scrubbed the pavements, in readiness. My mother stayed up all night to make flags on the sewing ma-

1935. Wharf Street Silver Jubilee party. Me, with Harry Holding from No. 8. Mother in check apron. Paint factory on left. Durham Arms, top left.

chine. She dyed my father's long-johns red at the top and blue at the bottom, leaving the centre white, and wore these to compete in the mum's race. All the neighbours cooperated to provide the food and entertain the children, who all wore fancy dress. There was much flag waving, of course. My mother was a staunch royalist, and so was I. When a year later, George the fifth lay dying, she again stayed up late into the night, to hear the bulletins on the radio. When at last he succumbed, she woke me up and in a trembling voice said, 'Ive.' (Ivy) 'He's gone!'

To celebrate the jubilee at school, we were all given a sixpenny piece in a commemorative envelope. Mr. Holding next door punched a hole in mine and I wore it round my neck. I have it to this day. We were asked to write a poem about the event. I was ten years old. I wrote:

> May the sixth. Jubilee
> The King is still alive.
> Oh, may he reign, so long again.
> Another twenty five.

Our teacher, 'Dolly' Dowling was ecstatic. She rushed into the next classroom, which was divided from ours by a curtain, and said to the teacher there, 'Look at this!' As a reward, I was put in charge of the jubilee scrap book, which was about three feet long, a task which I undertook enthusiastically. So diligent was I, that when I saw a picture of a crown on an advertising hoarding, near the station, I was eager to remove it. After a spell of very wet weather, I noticed that the paper was very sodden, and easily removable. During a heavy deluge, I left the house with a knife, and skillfully removed the crown. It was taken to school and proudly stuck on the front of the scrap book.

Dolly Dowling was an elderly teacher, or so she seemed. She was probably approaching retiring age. She was conscientious and must have had a difficult time coping with such a large class. There was always a long queue of children waiting to see her, either to get a piece of work marked, or to pick up a stitch, or to untangle a knot in the sewing thread. If we finished a set task too early, we had to be kept quiet somehow, and still-life drawing was a regular feature. On one occasion 'Dolly' hung a most luscious bunch of grapes on the wall and instructed us to draw them. I can see them now – a perfect bunch of tempting, large, dusky, blue grapes. With her head down, and the queue snaking past the mouth-watering grapes, one by one they were gradually removed. The pendulous bunch was turned round in an attempt to conceal the bare stalks. At play time, children sneaked in and finished them off, leaving just the stark 'skeleton' suspended on a string. Dolly could do nothing. Nobody owned up. We were all guilty. 'Oh well', she said, 'You'll have to draw from memory'. I still have that memory.

I was often given tasks at school to keep me quiet and when I skipped a class and remained in the final year for two years, I was particularly bored. To keep me occupied when I had finished a given piece of work too quickly, I was made to do some embroidery on a piece of hessian. I embroidered, 'D.D.' and 'Dolly' and 'S.F.D.' – Miss Dowling's initials which I had seen in the register. Sometimes I embroidered 'A.E.S.', the headmistress's initials. They must have known, but said nothing. Miss Stokes, the head teacher, would sometimes withdraw me from the class and take me to her room. I thought I had done something wrong, but I now realize she was giving me one-to-one coaching in preparation for the 'scholarship' exam.

In addition to the exam which we all sat at our own school, I was also asked to sit a separate exam for West Ham Grammar School. This had to be taken at the school itself and involved a tram ride and a walk. My mother accompanied me but she wasn't sure where it was and we arrived late. I was already nervous, but to compound matters, I worked with a very unreliable pen. The nib, which was scratchy anyway, kept falling out of the holder and dropping into the inkwell. After fishing it out, my fingers were very inky, and the blotting paper very damp. I think I spent more time coping with the mechanics of getting pen to paper than I did in giving any indication of my academic potential, or otherwise. I found my own way home and heard no more.

Incidentally, since I haven't mentioned this before, when I first learnt to write, I wrote with my left hand, like my father, and did 'mirror' writing. I recall my mother holding my writing up to the mirror, to decipher what I had written. I was forced to write with my right hand and also to hold a knife and fork in the socially acceptable manner. However, for most basic functions, I still use my left hand.

Fortunately, I was not a complete disappointment to A.E. Stokes and S.F. Dowling, as I was selected to attend the Russell Central School, in Queen's Road, Upton Park. This school had developed from the Russell Road Higher Elementary School, founded in 1906, but in 1932, a new school, Russell Central was built. This provided a four year secondary course, with artisans, rather than academics, in mind.

It was during the summer school holiday, in 1936, that I was called in off the street, and introduced to an official looking gentleman. My mother was heavily pregnant at the time, with her sixth child, Eddie, who was born in July. We must have appeared sufficiently poverty stricken, but no doubt worthy, for it was then that he sanctioned a grant of two pounds for a school uniform. I had a navy-blue blazer, a pleated gymslip, two blouses and a hat.

So, in 1936, suitably clothed in my new apparel, and going to a different school, I saw less of my Wharf Street and Stephenson Street friends. This was a pity. Even families were divided under this system of education, my own included. I know of many people for whom a comprehensive system of education would have opened up a whole new world.

This change of schooling, for me, however, proved to be one of the milestones in my life.

– 3 –

Secondary School Years and the Outbreak of War

In September 1936, I boarded the tram near Canning Town Station and journeyed to a new world. Russell school looked impressive, being only four years old. It provided a four year course and had a three form entry – one class for boys, one for girls and one mixed, so by today's standard, it was a small school, just twelve classes. It was built round an open quadrangle, with a sundial at the intersection of two crossed paths, used only by the teaching staff. The design was simple and therefore memorable, with cloakrooms at each short end of a rectangle, boys at one end, girls at the other. The hall, which was also the gymnasium, ran down the side facing the road. The classrooms occupied the other side, bordered on the outside by a paved terrace and flowerbeds. The terrace was raised above the playing field by a grassy bank and a short flight of steps at each end. We were forbidden to run down the bank, or to cycle along the terrace. The practical rooms, laboratories, domestic science and the art room were upstairs. We were given a tour of inspection and what impressed me was the surface of the stone floor of the corridor which surrounded the quadrangle and gave access to all the rooms alongside. It must have been speckled with fragments of quartz, as it glistened like diamonds. The whole appearance was a world apart from that of Canning Town Junior Mixed, built in 1877.

Newcomers assembled in the hall and were allotted to a form teacher. My class had a new teacher, Miss Banks, who was responsible for physical education and maths. She had us all lined up and checked that we were suitably uniformed, which we all were, except one poor unfortunate child. She really stood out! I immediately warmed to her. 'I'll see you later,' said Miss Banks. The rest of us were made to kneel on the hall floor to check that our tunics were five inches from the ground when kneeling. Mine was much too long as it was purchased 'to allow for growth' , so for some time it had a four inch hem. Irene's 'five inch' test took place a few days later, when after having provided an acceptable explanation for the absence of uniform, she came to school suitably attired. We became great friends.

My favourite lessons were the physical ones – P.T. (Physical Training), and Games, at which I had some success. As Miss Banks also taught maths, and I was anxious to impress, I scored here, too, and at the end of the first year was awarded the maths prize.

I 'blotted my copy book' at the first Domestic Science lesson, however. The subject being discussed was 'dining room etiquette' – how to position the knife and fork, etc. – and socially acceptable behaviour. We were repeatedly asked for suggestions. Hands kept shooting up. 'Yes' , said Miss Marchant. 'Any more?' There was no response. I tried to do my best and thought hard. I raised my hand. 'Miss! Miss!' 'Yes, child' . I was so pleased that I had been chosen and that I had an answer, and proudly announced, 'If you don't like the food, don't throw it under the table.' Oh, dear. Lesson number one. Think before you speak.

We also had 'Speech Training' lessons, with a very po-faced humourless teacher. We found these lessons hilarious and didn' t take them seriously. It was here that I was introduced to diphthongs. For weeks we went through a ritual of reciting diphthongs in staccato fashion and how to apply this exercise in pronunciation. It went like this:

      ee, oo,   ee, oo,   ee, oo,
      eeoo,   eeoo,   eeoo,

and then, starting on a high note, and coming down the scale,

      tune,   tune,   tune.

Likewise with:

      oy, ee,   oy, ee,   oy, ee,
      oyee,   oyee,   oyee,
      toil,   toil,   toil,

and so on, with uh, ee; uhee; time; and ay, ee; ayee; rain.

We then recited, 'I stood in Venice on the Bridge of Sighs... etc.' and then 'Radiant sister of the day, Awake, arise and come away, ... etc.' Another exercise was:

      The Duke paid the money, due to the Jew,
      Before the dew was off the grass on Tuesday,
      And the Jew, having duly acknowledged it,
      Said adieu to the Duke forever.'

We always wildly exaggerated the diphthongs and were able to pronounce them perfectly in the lesson. Something must have rubbed off on to us, as when we were entered for the Stratford and East London Musical Festival in 1938 and 1939, on each occasion I was awarded a first class certificate for elocution, and received applause from the school during morning assembly.

At home, I often had occasion to remember these lessons in speech training, quite humorously, in fact. To start the day, we had to go through the ritual of 'washing'. This took place in the cold scullery, standing in bare feet on the concrete floor. We used 'Sunlight' soap, which was also used for scrubbing floors, the back yard and the front step. It invariably had imbedded in it a few bristly fragments from the brush. There were four of us to get washed. My father would be in charge. He had a fetish for cleanliness. His mother and grandmother, after all, did run a laundry. The first one of us would wash and then shout, 'next,' and so on. We had to wash our feet by standing on one leg, raising the other, and placing the foot in the bowl in the sink. One morning, being in a hurry and afraid of being late for school, I omitted this exercise in gymnastic agility. He caught me, of course. Wait for it! 'Wash your fucking feet, you dirty bastard. You go to a fucking high school and can't wash your feet! Don't they teach you anything there?' 'Well,' I thought. 'I know my diphthongs and I can recite, 'The Duke paid the money due to the Jew,' but washing feet? No.' I said nothing – washed my feet, and was late for school.

Class sizes were smaller than at Bidder Street and for Domestic Science and Needlework, we were split. For 'D.S.' we each had a table with a large drawer containing a complete set of kitchen equipment. Food was cooked in a heating range built into the wall, with just one, or perhaps, two, gas cookers. One day we made sausage rolls and one girl lost her sausage. Some time was spent trying to locate it, to no avail, but when the sausage rolls came out of the oven, another pupil's were twice the size of everybody else's!

I enjoyed the needlework lessons. We first made a cookery apron with embroidered initials, and a school blouse. When we were measured, I had a twenty-eight inch bust, which gave rise to much mirth from my classmates. An on-going exercise was a 'sampler' , on which we practised various basic stitches, herringbone, chain, feather, stem, blanket and buttonhole. These had to be worked in straight lines, under supervision, a far cry from the freedom of expression I was able to exercise on the sack-like material in Dolly Dowling's class.

During my first year at the Russell School, I acquired a bicycle. This was actually purchased for Marie, who, at the age of thirteen, was 'selected' for admission to the newly-built Trade School for Girls, in Water Lane, Stratford. She opted for a cookery course. She was expected to cycle to school, but when, for some reason, she chose not to do so, my parents

First year at Russell Central School, 1937. A section from a panoramic photograph. Ivy Hicks is the sixth from the left on the front row.

were angry and gave it to me. So I was expected to cycle to school, which I was happy to do. I used to first cycle to Irene's house, on the other side of the railway, in Manor Road, and together we would complete the journey to school. I was often late in picking her up, but she always waited.

Homework was a new thing for me and very difficult to do at home. There was only one small table for eight of us and one small living room. It couldn't have been easy for most of us, but this dilemma was overcome. Arrangements were made for us to do our 'homework' at school, on three nights a week. When lessons finished at half past four, we had tea in the dining room, a wooden construction separate from the main building, on the edge of the playing field. We paid threepence for a cup of tea, a sandwich and a cake. From five to six o'clock we did our homework, supervised by a teacher. This was an excellent scheme and helped many of us to take advantage of the education offered.

About this time I began to have piano lessons given by a neighbour's relative, whose husband was killed in the First World War. She lived on the other side of the railway, over Peggy Leggy steps, and it seemed a long walk. I was provided with, what seemed then, a strange looking, very narrow, attaché case. As I walked along Stephenson Street, after school, I was often laughed at by children, or rather the case was. 'Here's that funny case, again,' they would say. When I arrived for my lesson, I would leave the sixpence on the piano. I was then given exercises to practise, whilst my tutor prepared tea for her family, who by this time were arriving home from work. It was a cold, bleak, front room. On the wall, on either side of the piano, were two pictures, 'The soldier's farewell' and 'The soldier's return'. The returning soldier had one leg missing. After this experience, I then had the long walk back home. When I practised on our piano in the cold front room, the boys from next door, or anybody else playing in the street, would tap on the window, and keep peering in. I didn't make much progress and eventually gave up, much to my mother's disappointment.

I settled in well at the new school and made many friends. School reports noted – 'Ivy works well, but is rather talkative in class' and 'With a little effort Ivy could be still higher in her form'. However, I was more interested in being popular with my friends than in being studious.

During the next few years, nothing much changed in Wharf Street. Older children left school at fourteen and went to work and a few more children were born, but that was all. Then towards the end of 1937, an event occurred which brought a modicum of excitement and interest to our family, for a few years at least. Unknowingly, we played a part in the 'plotlands' phenomenon, a movement that began in the early part of the twentieth century. It was then that the less affluent members of our society were able to purchase small freehold plots, on which, in the absence of planning controls, they were able to erect a holiday or retirement home. The first half of the twentieth century saw the emergence of these plots, particularly after the First World War. The agricultural depression, and the fact that many families with large estates had lost their sons in the war, increased the supply of land for sale. This was to change the landscape of southeast England, along the coast, on the riverside and in the country. To those on the outside of this development, the 'plotlands' , with their shacks, old trams and railway carriages, and makeshift constructions, were an eyesore. To the proud owners, however, a plot represented an escape from urban and inner-city pollution, a chance to organize one's own life, and something to look forward to, if only for an occasional weekend or a week in the summer. It gave one a purpose in life and satisfied the aspirations of many people who were living and working in an environment not of their choosing, but dictated by the aftermath of a rapidly expanding industrial society. They were, perhaps, even drawn back to the rural society they or their family had left only a generation or so ago.

Before the First World War, house ownership was beyond the reach of working-class people. Artisans and professional people in regular employment could aspire to house ownership, and some local authorities provided a limited amount of rented accommodation on housing estates, but there remained a large group of people who saw no prospect of improved living conditions. When redundant agricultural land came on the market, and plots ranging from £10 to £50 – with easy terms – were available, it was from this group that the 'plotlanders' came. Sadly, even a plot seemed beyond our dreams. However, by an accident of history, our family fortune was to change.

In November, brother Lawrie was seventeen, and after shopping for a gift, mother boarded a tram along the Barking Road. As she was alighting, the tram took off. She tripped and broke her arm. Unfortunate you may think. Painful, certainly; but a blessing in disguise. Having placed a regular order with the newsagent for the 'News of the World', she was entitled to free accident insurance. She made a claim and was awarded £40 – a small fortune. This was the chance of a lifetime to broaden her horizons and was not to be missed.

A frequent visitor to Wharf Street was my father's bachelor cousin, Fred Hicks, who always called on Boxing Day and Easter Sunday, with a small gift. He was just two years younger than my father and there was a striking similarity in their appearance. But here, the similarity ended. 'Uncle' Fred was relaxed and easy-going, friendly and gentle and never raised his voice in anger. Would my father have been like this, without 'the boxing', I wonder? I could not understand why Uncle Fred had never married. He had lived with the same 'landlady' and her husband since he was a young man. And thereby hangs a tale. But I digress. At the time of my mother's 'small fortune', Uncle Fred had a small bungalow on a plot at Hook End, near Blackmore, in Essex. He had been brought up in Manor Road, West Ham, but had now returned to the countryside of his forebears and worked as a gardener-handyman at Kelvedon Hall. He learned that a local farmer was selling off some economically unproductive land, in plots, and advised my mother to purchase one. This was a big step to take. Never before having made such a large financial transaction she was hesitant, but did attend the auction where she was too nervous to make a bid. A small number of plots went 'under the hammer' at ten shillings (50p) per foot frontage. The next day, after consultation with Uncle Fred, she bought one of these plots for 12/6d per foot. Thus, she became the proud owner of a plot of land 40 feet by about 150 feet. I am not sure of the exact depth, but it was certainly long. The plot had cost her £25. This was 1937.

This plot was not typical of the plots which created Jaywick, Peacehaven, Canvey Island, Pitsea, Laindon and many others. It was a smaller scale development and we were not far removed from public transport. A trolleybus to Stratford, then a Green Line coach to Brentwood and a single-decker bus to Hook End and we were in another world. We were fortunate in that Uncle Fred was available to lend us tools and give us advice. During the Spring of 1938, we acquired a large wooden shed which served as our living room, and a caravan which slept five people. We obtained water from a standpipe. My mother built a very fine tool shed; this was when I first heard the expression 'tongue and groove'. Adjoining the shed was the toilet, a primitive bucket arrangement which was emptied at frequent intervals into a deep hole dug at the end of the plot. We cooked on an oil stove with a 'Dutch oven' on top for the Sunday roast. Oil lamps provided the lighting.

The adjacent plots were not occupied at the time, but the one 'next door' had an old tram on it in which we played for hours. My mother had our plot fenced and called it 'Benares', not the sacred place in India, I'm afraid, but after Benares Road, Plumstead, where she lived as a child! I was thirteen years old at the time and with Marie, aged fourteen and Jimmy aged eleven, we roamed the countryside for hours. We picked blackberries and mushrooms, and armed with sticks, followed the harvester cutting the wheat, hoping at the end to kill one of the rabbits trapped in the un-reaped crop in the centre. We never did. We made daisy chains and learned how to draw water from a well. We heard the cuckoo for the first time and enriched our vocabulary with words such as spinney, copse and meadow, and even 'Saxon church'. All a far cry from life in Canning Town.

For a time we continued to enjoy our Shangri-La, unaware of the deepening political crisis. During that autumn of 1938, our main concern was to see who could gather the most blackberries to turn into jam, but our politicians had other concerns. Whilst our territorial ambitions extended no further than 'Benares', the German government had designs on Czechoslovakia, and when their plans seemed to threaten British interests, a second war with Germany seemed a possibility. Only twenty years had elapsed since the end of the last war and painful memories of the Somme and other battlefields were still fresh in the minds of many. We children were not in a position to appreciate the seriousness of the situation and were quite excited by the preparations being made for our welfare. Arrangements were made for children, invalids and expectant mothers to be evacuated from London, and meetings were held in schools to explain the situation. Gas masks began to be issued with instructions given for their use. We tried them on and I remember they smelt very rubbery and made breathing difficult. They were supplied in a box and gas mask cases became a fashion accessory. My mother quickly made attractive bags for us which we slung round our shoulder. Information was spread by radio announcements and people made sure the batteries on their sets did not run out and kept the accumulators topped up. I do remember there was much relief when the Prime Minister, Chamberlain, returned from Germany that September, and announced, 'There will be peace in our time'.

So the halcyon days on our 'plot' continued into 1939, except for Jimmy, whose freedom to explore was cut short in June. For some time he had been complaining of pains in his hip, and when he had not been seen for several hours, we became concerned. He was then discovered in the outside toilet, doubled up in agony and unable to move. 'Growing pains,' said my father. 'I'll see to that.' Whereupon he was placed on the table and massaged with his 'white oils', which he considered to be a panacea for all aches and pains, based on his long experience of dealing with boxers' muscular injuries. Poor Jimmy screamed in agony and it was obvious something was wrong. As was usually the case in emergencies, a visit to Poplar Hospital was suggested. He was put into Eddie's pushchair and I pushed him over the 'iron bridge', and along the East India Dock Road to Poplar Hospital. We didn't make appointments in those days. We just turned up. I asked for Jimmy to be seen and he was. I waited for some time and eventually was told that he needed to be kept in and to be operated on. 'Where's your mother?' they said. When I said that she had gone shopping, I was told to fetch her immediately as they could not proceed without her consent. I returned home but she had not yet arrived, so I proceeded towards Rathbone Street. I met her coming along Barking Road. She had combined the shopping trip with a visit to the hairdresser's for a Marcel wave, a common way then of waving the hair with curling tongs heated on a gas jet. She ran all the way to the hospital and Jimmy was operated on immediately. He had osteomyelitis of the upper femur, quite a serious condition then and not treatable by antibiotics. The infection in the bone marrow could only be reached by removing a section of the bone. This condition caused him much pain and discomfort for many years. This was the second time that removal of a section of bone had saved his life. When he was about two years old he suffered from empyema, a condition often fatal in a child so young. On that occasion, for some reason, pus, or an abscess, had developed in the pleural cavity, the space between the lungs and the chest wall. To drain the pus, a section of rib had to be removed. He still has a large, deep scar below his shoulder blade.

Throughout the summer, the prospect of war with Germany became ever more likely. Again there were meetings at schools and parents were advised to put all their children's names down for evacuation, 'or suffer the consequences'. Mothers began to argue with each other. 'I'm not parting with my children,' was a plea frequently heard. 'If we're going to die, we'll all die together.' Some mothers were accused of parting with their children too readily, who then replied, 'If you loved your children, you'd let them go.' It was a sad time for mothers and many families were split, never to be united as a family again.

That September proved to be a watershed in the lives of the Hicks family of Wharf Street, for better or for worse. Lawrie was approaching nineteen, and was very soon conscripted into the Royal Army Service Corps. He was sent to France with the British Expeditionary Force in January, 1940. Marie and I, at sixteen and fourteen, were at different schools and Jimmy was still in Poplar Hospital and later sent to their convalescent home at Walton-on-the-Naze. It was decided that in the event of evacuation, Marie and I, and Patricia aged six years, should remain together. This meant that I had to leave my friends at the Russell School and attach myself to Marie's school. This was the saddest blow of all. Going away with all my friends and teachers seemed an attractive idea. Eddie, aged three, was at the local nursery school and it was decided that the whole school would be transferred to Bishops Stortford, to the large country house belonging to the mother of one of the teachers.

So, on the 1st September, we said good-bye to our beloved, happy, little brother, who thought it was just another day, and would be collected at three o' clock as usual. Nothing was explained to him – perhaps he was too young – but I now believe he was psychologically damaged by that separation. I would certainly not have parted with a three-year-old child, particularly one who, as the youngest of a large family, had been so very much fussed over and loved.

Marie, Pat and I, said goodbye to neighbours and friends and went to Marie's school, the West Ham Trade School for Girls, in Water Lane, Stratford. Nobody had any idea where we might be going. We waited at the school for the whole day and were then sent home and told to report the next day. The atmosphere in Wharf Street when we returned was very sombre. George, next door, said that during the day, the street was deathly quiet, with no children running about. 'It was strange,' he said. 'Mothers stood at their front doors and just stared.' War had not then been declared, so nobody knew what to expect.

The next day, the three of us again set off, having had another bath, at great inconvenience. The zinc bath was unhooked from the back-yard wall and placed in the kitchen. Saucepans of water were heated on the gas stove and emptied into the bath and we each had a turn. We departed, complete with gas masks, and nothing much more than the clothes we stood up in. 'Don't forget,' said mother. 'Keep together! You are not to be split up!'

We had expected to go on a train journey and were quite surprised when coaches arrived to take us to our secret destination. We settled down for a long journey, and as we pulled out of Stratford, Marie and I found we were familiar with the route. We thought we were on the way to Romford, and so it proved. We had many times done the journey by Greenline coach to Brentwood, on the way to Blackmore. Imagine our surprise when we did actually reach Brentwood. If only we could have got out there, and taken the little bus to Hook End, and 'Benares'. Instead, we went on to Chelmsford, our destination. There we were herded into groups and deposited at streets along Broomfield Road, First Avenue, Second Avenue, and so on, up to Eighth Avenue. The roads had recently been constructed but houses were still being built in Seventh and Eighth Avenue. We were with a group deposited on a grass verge in Fifth Avenue, to await selection. It was reminiscent of a cattle market, or slave auction. People would point, 'I'll have that one. No, not that one. The one to the left,' and so on. Pretty little Patricia would have gone very early on, but we hung on to her. She came with a package. 'Take Pat and you take the two ugly sisters' sort of thing. Needless to say, as darkness fell, we three were still sitting on the grass verge, everybody else having been selected. We were indeed a problem, which was eventually solved by a saintly couple acting for the love of god, rather than for the love of three very tired and hungry evacuees from the East End of London. The Nortons were recently married, with a new home and Mr. Norton was a lay preacher. The first thing they said was, 'Get in the bath, and wash your hair.' To which I replied, 'But we did that this morning', a remark which probably gave the opposite impression to what I intended.

Those first few weeks in Chelmsford were pretty miserable. War was declared the day after we arrived. On that day the air raid siren went and we all escaped to the air-raid shelter, clutching our gas masks, but it was a false alarm. Schooling had not yet begun as arrangements had to be made to share premises with the local school and it was a month before half-day schooling was organised. We spent mornings on the playing fields or in the gymnasium and afternoons in the classroom.

Soon after we arrived we had to keep a daily record and hand it in to the teacher responsible for us. I still have mine to this day. It is certainly no literary gem, but it does indicate that Marie and I did quite a lot for ourselves and that the Nortons were cold and unfeeling. We laid and cleared the table and washed up for all meals, which we had separately from the Nortons. We prepared the vegetables, did our own washing, ironing and mending, cleaned our bedroom and the windows and went to Church twice on Sunday. We had complete responsibility for Pat. A typical entry reads, 'Thursday, 21st September. After breakfast, I cleared the table and washed up. Did half the vegetables and then made my bed. I went into every grocery shop possible to get some sugar. Arrived home with twelve pounds.' The next day, Friday, 22nd September. 'Did my usual routine. Did my own and Pat's washing. Noon – Helped to lay the table. After dinner I cleared away and washed up. Ironed mine and Pat's gas-mask cases. Went to town with Mrs. Norton. Evening – After coming back from market, I laid the table, cut some bread and made some tea. Ironed the clothes and helped clean the windows.' There was a lighter note on Tuesday the 26th. 'Received a letter from Mum, which contained ten shillings for shoe repairs, wool for jumpers, and pocket money.' We must have purchased the knitting wool, because on Thursday evening, the 28th, 'We went to Mrs. Chittock's house. I spent a very enjoyable evening round the fire and doing knitting. Olive Cox made some toffee apples. We all watched and afterwards had one each. We looked at the clock and it was 8.45 and Pat was not in bed. We had not realized. The time had simply flown. Marie took Pat in and came back crying. Mr. Norton had grumbled at her for being so late and simply jumped down her throat.'

In spite of the fact that we were not at all happy there, it did not occur to us to return home. We knew the way. It was only a couple of hours and a coach ride away. We were teenagers and quite capable of looking after ourselves, but we knew our parents would disapprove. There was the fear, then, of course, that Londoners might be gassed, or bombed, and anyway, we had Pat to look after. A friend of Marie's, however, had no such qualms. She was so miserable that she decided, without reference to her parents, to return home. She sought Marie's help, and Marie lent her the fare and explained the journey to her. It was then left to Marie to explain her absence.

Things did improve later, when Marie and Pat moved in with the kindly Mrs. Chittock, who already had two evacuees and two children of her own. They were very happy there. For some weeks, I had been calling at houses, asking, 'Do you want an evacuee?' I was eventually taken in by Mrs. Burrows, who lived opposite the Chittocks, and joined my friend Maud who was already there. She was a kindly but neurotic woman, with a 'saint' of a husband, and we were too much for her. She complained that we were taking baths together and made too much noise. After two weeks we had to move on and were taken in by a family, the Lakins, with whom we had become friendly. There were seven boys and one girl, Jean, the youngest. Five boys and Jean were still at home. The dining table had three and a half legs and books took the place of the missing half. Poor Jean, aged twelve, had to share her bed with Maud and me, and it wasn't very wide, either. We were happy there and often went to football matches with Mr. Lakin and the boys. Mrs. Lakin was a large woman, who had 'internal trouble', and was often confined to an armchair, but we were never made to feel unwelcome, and everybody helped around the house.

Meanwhile, back in London, nothing much was happening. It was the period of the 'phoney' war and evacuees began to return. Maud returned home in December and I returned home just before Christmas. Marie and Pat happily stayed with Mrs. Chittock.

At the beginning of 1940, schools in West Ham began to re-open. Although the war had not been 'over by Christmas' as many had predicted, there was a more relaxed attitude generally. I was delighted when I heard that the Russell school was to open, and I couldn't return quickly enough. I wondered who else would be there. The number of pupils was considerably reduced, as of course was the staff, with an acting headmaster. He was much more approachable and likeable than the permanent head, an unsympathetic, 'cold fish' of a man, whose name, inappropriately, was C.W.Truelove. He did return a few months later.

The next two terms at school were very happy ones. I was pleased to find Irene there, and we spent many happy days cycling to Epping Forest. We were not stretched academically. I remember long periods of physical activity, playing netball, rounders and stool ball, and in fine weather the breaks were longer than the regulation fifteen minutes. This was in fact my fourth year of secondary education. The first term was spent at Chelmsford, and was a waste of time from an educational point of view. I had been placed in the Commerce department, where Spanish was taught instead of the French I had been learning. I was faced with bookkeeping lessons, with balance sheets, profit and loss accounts, stocks and shares, etc. which I did not warm to at all. We had typing lessons, where all the keys were covered up, to encourage the correct fingering, and to stop us from looking at the keys. The shorthand was Pitman's and not Gregg, which I had commenced. So with a very relaxed further two terms at Russell, I had received virtually only three years of secondary education. What I did pick up from my days at the Russell school, however, was a love of, and, indeed, thirst for education, which served me in good stead in the years to come.

Marie was more fortunate, in that she was able to continue with her cookery course in Chelmsford. Whilst Pat returned home early in 1940, Marie was advised to remain and to study for a City and Guilds certificate. West Ham was a generous Education Authority, and we both had a grant to enable us to remain at school. The school leaving age was then fourteen, but if we remained at school, there was a means tested allowance of £1 per month, which we both received. Fifteen shillings of my pound went to my mother, and I received five shillings. Marie was successful in the City and Guilds examination, and then returned home.

This semblance of normality was not to last. We didn't know quite what was happening, but in May the eight months of relative inactivity came to an end and the war began in earnest. I was oblivious to the seriousness of the situation and had arranged to stay at 'Benares' with Irene and three other friends during the Whitsun holiday. Permission from their parents had been obtained, and when all the parties were satisfied that we could be trusted to act sensibly, we made plans for the 'adventure of a lifetime'. Then came the bad news. The Whitsun school holiday was cancelled. Events in Europe had taken a turn for the worst. Germany had taken over Denmark and most of the airfields and ports of Norway, and the future looked bleak. Schools once again were to be used as assembly points should evacuation be necessary. However, we decided to proceed with our plans, in the belief that we would be safer in Essex than in London.

We cycled to Hook End on Saturday the 11th, and prepared for a glorious week. I was keen to introduce Irene, Lily, Beaty and Olive, to the pleasures of the Essex countryside. We were very well organised and enjoyed shopping for and cooking our meals. We took turns to be responsible for the catering for a day and the arrangement worked well. I checked the blackout every night and kept overall supervision, 'like a clucking hen', they said. We gave no thought to the political situation, but that week Holland surrendered and Churchill took over from Chamberlain, promising 'Nothing, but blood, toil, tears and sweat.'

On the Thursday, after a very exhilarating day out, we returned in high spirits to the 'chalet', or more precisely, the large shed, to find that my father had been there and left a note. It read, 'You are to return home immediately.' I thought the war had taken a serious turn, but nothing of the sort. The note continued, 'You have not kept the bowls clean and you were seen talking to two airmen by the spinny. Come home at once.' Well, of course, then I always obeyed my father, so the following day we packed up and cycled home, sadly on a sour note, rather than the excitement we had been feeling at having snatched a memorable holiday, whilst all around was doom and gloom.

We returned to school the following Monday, in fear and trembling, at having disobeyed orders. We were sent for by the acting Headmaster, 'Dicky Deighton'. With a grave expression he asked us to account for our absence the previous week. I explained that we had booked a holiday and, not wishing to lose our deposit, we kept to our plans. He seemed interested and asked if we had enjoyed the holiday. The next day at the morning assembly, we were called up on to the stage. We were then congratulated for cocking a snook at Hitler. 'These five girls made the brave

June 1940. In garden at Wharf Street. Note Anderson shelter at end of garden.

decision not to allow Hitler to change their plans. They were not afraid. We can all learn from their attitude. Whatever happens in the coming weeks, let us all show the same determination and spirit. Well done, girls!' After which, we were loudly clapped and regarded as heroines.

Events had however taken a serious turn. When Luxembourg, Holland and Belgium fell, it looked as though Churchill's promise would be fulfilled. It was decided to retreat from France as soon as possible. Then began the evacuation from Dunkirk. It was presented to us at that time as a great achievement, and a kind of victory, whereas now we still see it as a fine achievement, but on the coat tails of a great disaster. And there still remained thousands of British troops cut off in France. Evacuation where possible continued throughout June and another two hundred thousand were brought back. Many made their way to St. Nazaire. My brother Lawrie and my father's second from youngest brother, Horace, were caught up in all this. In Lawrie's detailed account of the period, he portrays a scene of confusion, where one's survival depended on chance factors. In his case, very much so.

When he had gone with the B.E.F. to France in January, he was sent to a camp at Pornichet where units were based which were used to unload supplies at St. Nazaire. When later they were sent north-east, by a train normally used for transporting cattle, he failed to report for roll call at the end of the journey. He was reported missing and a telegram was sent to my mother to this effect. It was twenty-four years since her brother Fred was reported missing and there was no happy ending on that occasion. However, back in France, Lawrie was discovered, still on the straw in the truck, where he had lain unconscious for three days. He was taken by stretcher to Dieppe, where he was found to be suffering from cerebro-spinal meningitis. The rest of his unit moved on and were eventually captured.

By the time friends and relatives arrived to commiserate with us, a second telegram had been received to the effect that Lawrie was no longer missing and could be visited in hospital. Such optimism! No flowers or grapes were taken to Lawrie, for, as the Germans advanced towards the Channel ports, all traffic was one way. Troops were now making for Dunkirk and Dieppe was under attack. Lawrie, and the other convalescing soldiers there, in their hospital 'blues', had to defend the cliff-top against parachutists with pickaxe handles, firearms not being allowed under the Geneva Convention, for invalids.

There was understandably great excitement and euphoria when soldiers returned from Dunkirk, but there were still thousands of British troops south of the Somme and their families could not rejoice. It was several weeks before some of these made their way to Cherbourg and St.

Nazaire, where Lawrie eventually arrived. He recalls that when they reached St. Nazaire they found trucks blazing or being made unusable. There were miles of dispirited and tired soldiers slowly moving along in the hope of getting a boat at the Docks. Most were still in their units with their officers. When the officer in charge of his small group said 'Every man for himself,' he made his way to the Dock front. Another person who was there, was Fred Stanley. I wrote to him recently, after reading a letter he had written to the local paper. In reply he stated:

> The situation was very confused and in fact, a large French ship called the 'Champlain', was still discharging twin-engined Douglas bombers from America and British stevedore groups were doing the discharging. I was Able Seaman on an old British cargo vessel called the 'Dundrum Castle' We were bound for Dunkirk from South Africa when we were diverted to St. Nazaire to assist in the evacuation of the remainder of the British forces. The 'Lancastria' was anchored outside and crammed with troops, which were being ferried out to her by tenders. At about 2 o' clock in the afternoon, 'Lancastria' was bombed and sank immediately, throwing five or six thousand men into the sea, which was covered in black fuel oil.

In his opinion more lives could have been saved if action had been taken more quickly and more efficiently.

Lawrie, fortunately, with several thousand others, boarded the Polish liner, the 'Stefan Batory', and after nearly three days of weaving about at sea arrived at Plymouth – four weeks after Dunkirk. Uncle Horace, my father's brother, was not so fortunate. Thirty-seven at the outbreak of war and being in the Territorial Army, he was called up immediately. He, too, was at St. Nazaire. My brother Lawrie, in a letter he wrote to me about that day, stated that:

> Uncle Horace was on the 'Lancastria'. The last that I saw of it was at an angle of 90 degrees, disappearing beneath the sea after being bombed. It was about a quarter of a mile away from us. Uncle Horace was a good swimmer but was one of the hundreds on the ship that were killed. It might just as well have been us, but we were lucky. Incidentally Lizzy Brown's husband was also on the 'Lancastria' but managed to get out alive. I met him and Lizzy some months after by chance in the Liverpool Arms at Canning Town. We had a couple of drinks together and relived that terrible night.

At the time, there were many ships close by and it remains a mystery why more men were not picked up. The Master of the 'Lancastria' later testified that, 'No panic occurred.' This 'lack of panic' was no consolation to Horace's widow and his four children.

At home, we knew very little about the progress of the war in France and the disasters taking place. There was no television, internet or email and news was slow to spread. We did know, however, that the situation was sufficiently serious for children to be evacuated again. Patricia, then aged seven, was sent to Devon to be with the Bidder Street School. Nearly fifty years later, we paid a visit to Umberleigh, the Devonshire village where she had stayed. She had since moved to Canada and this was her first visit. She told me how desperately unhappy she had been. Having arrived in Devon after the rest of the school, she was placed in a different village. She knew nobody and couldn't understand why she had been taken away from home. For several nights, she cried herself to sleep. Fortunately, her hosts, Mr. and Mrs. Boucher, were an elderly couple who had already raised a large family and were very kind and understanding. She stayed there until 1943, when it was thought she should return home, in readiness for the 'eleven plus' examination, as it was expected that she would gain a grammar school place. By then she had become very attached to the Bouchers and sadly missed village life and country ways on her return to West Ham.

When Pat was sent to Devon, Jimmy, aged thirteen was sent to be with his school, in Somerset. He was thought to be sufficiently recovered from osteomyelitis. So he, too, suffered a further upheaval. Eddie remained at the nursery school at Bishops Stortford. Perhaps Marie and I were the lucky ones. Marie continued her education at Chelmsford and I continued for a few months longer at the Russell School.

Towards the end of term, which then continued well into August, we were occupied with the thought of getting jobs. We had no 'school certificates' or matriculation qualifications, or anything the equivalent of today's GCEs. We were told that our chance of getting a job was dependent on the headmaster's testimonial and our scholastic attainment. This was measured by an examination in English and Commercial Arithmetic, set by the Royal Society of Arts and also the London School of Commerce. Vacancies were sent to the school and were handed out. We were given advice about an interview, which in effect told us to be clean, tidy, polite and respectful. I shall always remember a different sort of advice given to me by the Geography master, Dr. Reg. Morris. 'There will be several candidates for the job,' he said. 'You will be asked how much you expect to be paid. The best you can expect is twenty five shillings, (£1.25p). You are all to ask for this sum. Do not ask for less, or the job will go to the lowest bidder. This is called 'wage cutting' and helps to keep wages down.' This was the best advice I received as I embarked on the 'world of work.'

I was sent to a firm in Aldersgate, called Essenbee Products Ltd. 'Essenbee' stood for 'screws and bolts'. I found my own way there, by bus, and was duly interviewed for the post of 'Invoice Clerk', along with a few other girls from school. I obtained the post at a wage of twenty-five shillings. We must have all heeded Dr. Morris's advice. Thank you Dr. Morris. I left school the next day, in tears at it happened, at the thought of leaving all my friends, and started work straight away.

My final school year had been a strange one, starting with the outbreak of war, followed by evacuation and the break up of the family, never to meet as a family again. France had fallen and it looked as though it would be quite a few Christmases before the war was over. Jimmy, Pat, Eddie and Lawrie were still away, all in different places and not in communication with each other. This situation was not unusual then. Brothers and sisters led different lives, and in many cases close family ties failed to develop. Yet another casualty of war. The four years since I started at the Russell School seemed a lifetime away. There had been many changes but there were more to come.

This was taken the week I left school.

– 4 –

The Blitz, and Farewell to Wharf Street

At the end of August 1940, I started work, rather timidly, carrying a few sandwiches for lunch and a gas mask in a case which doubled up as a handbag. I caught a bus near Canning Town Station which took me over the Iron Bridge, along East India Dock Road and Commercial Road. My memory fails me at this point. What I do remember is the unusual smell of 'Essenbee' products. It was a mixture of metal, lubricating oil and varnish. Sixty years later, the smell of varnish still reminds me of my first day at work.

I had very little time to develop my skills as an invoice typist, or to become acquainted with the world of screws and bolts. My first week of paid employment coincided with the first week of German air raids. On several occasions the air raid siren sounded and we all went to a basement shelter, with the shop-floor workers separated from the office staff. I found this rather uncomfortable, as I identified more with the lively manual workers than with the more reserved office staff.

After little more than a week, on September 7th, and ten days before my sixteenth birthday, I met up with my school friend Rene. We were pleased to meet again and decided to go on a cycle trip. That day proved one to remember, and one which I recorded at the time. I later used the diary entry to write an article for the Newham History Society Newsletter. I repeated it verbatim, just as I wrote it then. It illustrated what I believed and thought about that memorable day, and read:

> As we have been kept in most of the week, owing to the air raids, Irene and I decided to go out cycling in the country. We thought we would go to Epping Forest. This we were warned against as the Germans had said they would set Epping Forest alight, because our Air Force had recently dropped bombs in the Black Forest, and set a good portion of it alight. However we decided to take the risk and set off in good spirits. When we were in Epping Forest the air raid siren went. Nobody took much notice as the raids had not been very intense. From the Forest we could see hundreds of planes crossing to London. We thought these were British, but apparently they were Jerries. Many

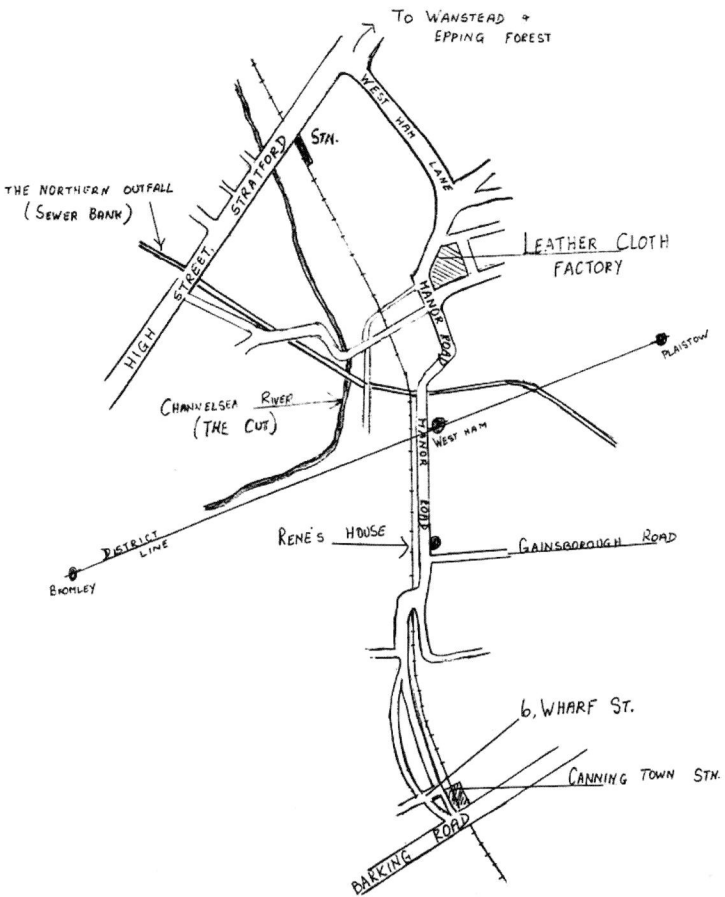

Sketch map showing the location of the last part of our hazardous cycle ride home after a day in Epping Forest on the first day of the Blitz, 7th September 1940.

air battles were going on and there was plenty of gunfire. We saw five planes brought down and saw several airmen bale out. Rene and I chased off on our bikes to try to find them, but soldiers were on the scene before us. Shrapnel was falling everywhere, so we sheltered under trees for protection. When things seemed quieter we decided to go home and the 'All Clear' sounded when we reached Wanstead at 6pm. As we approached London we could see huge black smoke clouds and thought we were in for a storm. We later discovered it was smoke from the many fires started by bombs. Damage became more severe as we approached home, and on arriving at Stratford, everything seemed to be burning. To get home we had to go by the

Leather Cloth factory but we could not get near it as it was on fire. We could not get near home at all as we were turned back by policemen. Eventually we made a detour and went along by a canal (the Cut) at the back of the factories. Most of these were on fire and we were both drenched with water from the firemen's hoses.

From the Cut we arrived at the sewer bank and walked along this until we reached West Ham Station, which was badly damaged. Nobody seemed to be about and as we went to get to Rene's house we were stopped and told by a Warden that a time bomb was in her front garden. In fact there were time bombs all along the route we had taken from Stratford. After some time we found Rene's family in Gainsborough Road School with a lot of other families waiting for time bombs to explode. I was not allowed to leave the school as it was rather dangerous. Two hours later, after much persuasion, I was allowed to try to get home (if it was still there). Rene's brother Eric accompanied me and, after taking many detours, I eventually arrived home. Mum had been very worried and practically bit my head off, giving me no time to explain. She said I was NOT to go out any more. I had been in about five minutes when another raid began and we all spent the night in the Anderson shelter. Bombs dropped all night and the sky was red for miles around with the glare of fires. We learned later that on that night an invasion of Britain was attempted. All Home Guard were on duty and all forces on the alert. Cousin George, in the Navy, said that as the Germans attempted to cross the Channel petrol was poured on the water and set alight. Those that were not burned turned back. Thousands of civilians were killed in the air raid. [Actually official statistics give a much lower figure.]

Reading the account now, I marvel at our survival. On that unforgettable day, September 7th, we had set out in high spirits, to enjoy a day in Epping Forest. We witnessed air battles taking place and airmen baling out. We sheltered under trees to escape the shrapnel. We thought all the action was taking place there. 'We'll have something to tell them back home,' we said. In fact, we nearly didn't reach home, with falling debris from blazing factories and our route littered with time bombs. Had it not been for Rene knowing her way about, we may never have reached home. At Stratford, every way we turned, we were sent back. I was certainly confused, but Rene lived fairly close by, in Manor Road, and was able to pick her way around. I do remember crying, not from fear, but from frustration. I wanted to get home but couldn't. 'No, you can't get through there. Time bombs! No, not there. The road's blown up.' We had to go somewhere, but it seemed that we couldn't go anywhere. By devious means we reached a narrow stretch of water, which Rene knew as The Cut, but is now certainly known as the 'Channelsea'. We cycled alongside it until we reached the sewer bank, or to be more precise, the Northern Outfall. From there, we reached Manor Road, where Rene lived. Her house backed on to Gainsborough Road School playground. Rene's family were sheltering at the school and I had to wait there for several hours before I was allowed out, as the area was surrounded by time bombs. Rene's brother Eric helped me to get home, which wasn't easy. The road to Stephenson Street was blocked and the pedestrian bridge at Peggy Leggy steps had a hole in it. We both had bicycles too. Looking back, we did remarkably well to reach Wharf Street. Was my mother pleased? If she was, she had a funny way of showing it. To use an expression an 'eastender' would recognise, 'We got a right mouthful.' Eric had risked his life to get me home only to face an onslaught for his pains. I did not see him again for 59 years, at Rene's Golden Wedding reunion. He vividly remembered the occasion and said, 'Your mother really laid into me.' As a result of meeting me again after all those years, Eric was prompted to send me an account of his memories of that day. It is such a marvellously vivid account, and a valuable addition to my own memories, that I have included it in its entirety, as an appendix.

That day, September 7th, 1940, was the first and only time I had been along the Cut, until one hot day in July, 59 years later. I had heard about the Lower Lea Project, a scheme which includes the creation of 'greenways' and the development of 'heritage' areas in that part of the river Lea. I went with my husband John to rediscover this part of my past. We found ourselves walking along an attractive, shrub-lined path and a display board informed us that this was in fact the 'Channelsea Path' and had once been a water-way and was filled in to create the footpath. This path led us to the 'Greenway', which was in fact our sewer bank. I was thrilled to discover all this, and a lump came to my throat as I recalled that day with Rene. It made me more determined than ever to write down the events of that dreadful day. Would anybody looking around now believe me? I didn't dream it. It really did happen. Rene now lives in Cornwall, but I will take her along the Channelsea Path one day.

I recorded those events shortly after they took place. However, many rumours circulated during the war as we were kept in some ignorance of the state of affairs. War historians would perhaps be able to assess their authenticity. Was an invasion attempted on 7th September, as we believed? Was cousin George correct when he said that invading Germans were burnt to death by petrol being poured on the English Channel? Was there a plan to destroy Epping Forest by fire? What we do know now is that September 7th marked the beginning of the blitz on London, which was heavily bombed every night except one, until November 14th. On the first day, 350 German bombers with an escort of more than 600 fighters, crossed the Channel in two waves. Canning Town and Silvertown bore the brunt of the attack, the main targets being the Beckton Gasworks, the Docks and the Woolwich Arsenal.

My mother's brother, Herbert Homes, was living in Plumstead at the time, in Benares Road, in my mother's former home. He was employed at Tate and Lyle's, North Woolwich, and had been a part-time volunteer of the A.F.S. since 1938. He was Company Officer on the night of the 7th and was in great demand. As a result of his action in fighting a fire at the Woolwich Arsenal, he received a Commendation for his services. His son, my cousin Bert, still has the letter informing him of the award, dated 27th February, 1941. It reads:

> I am directed by the Minister of Home Security to inform you that the Chairman of the London County Council drew his attention to your gallant conduct on 7th September, 1940, when your organization of the water supply rendered valuable assistance in fighting a fire at the Royal Arsenal, Woolwich. Mr. Herbert Morrison felt your resource and initiative were deserving of high praise and he took steps to bring the matter to the notice of his Majesty the King. I now have the pleasure of informing you that His Majesty has been graciously pleased to give orders for the publication of your name as having received an expression of Commendation for your services.
>
> The notice will appear in a list to be published as a Supplement to the London Gazette on the evening of Friday, 23rd September, 1941.

My diary continued the following day, Sunday, 8th of September:

> I called to see Rene but her home was destroyed when the time bomb exploded. I went to Gainsborough Road School, but she was not there. Some neighbours told me that she was staying with relatives and gave me her address. That night London was again heavily bombed and thousands killed.

Many years later, Rene also wrote an account of that day:

> I can confirm the happenings on that day just as Ivy recorded them in her diary and can continue from where I apparently disappeared from the scene. At the Gainsborough Road School that night we watched the horrendous firework display of incendiary bombs and the flashes

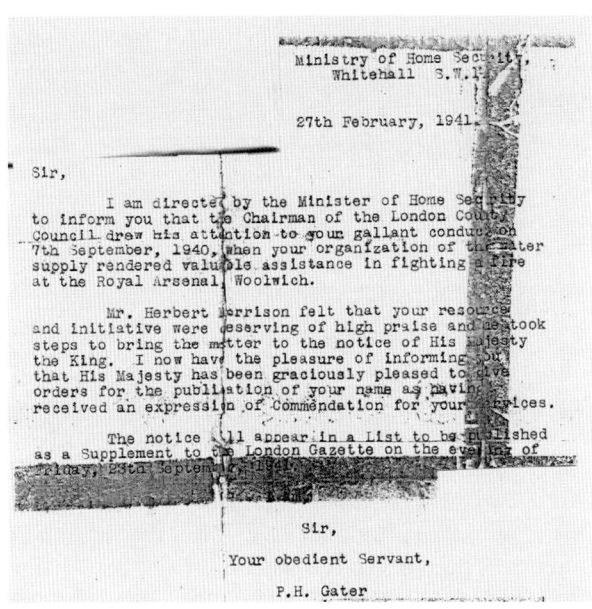

Company Officer Herbert Homes.

Mother's brother Bert, and the part he played during the Blitz.

from the guns going off all round, and then with a great noise and explosion, our house, which backed onto the school playground received its death sentence.

They spent a few days with various brothers – Rene had seven – and after being 'bombed out' three times Rene and her mother went to Chulmleigh, in Devon.

The next day, Monday, I set out for work as usual, and was amazed at the devastation I saw all around. It certainly had been a very bad night, with the sky lit up by huge fires and the frightening sound of exploding bombs. Apart from the destruction I saw when making my way home from Epping Forest, I had not seen any other large-scale damage. Somehow, my mind had not yet adjusted to the situation and I set out from home expecting to get a bus as usual. How wrong I was. Buildings and vehicles were bombed and there was debris scattered everywhere. Roads were impassable. I should have turned back, but I kept walking, hoping to catch a bus at some point. I picked my way along, all the way to Aldersgate. I don't know how many miles it was, but it seemed a long way. When I arrived at work, I apologised for being late! There wasn't much work done that day, and I was allowed home a little earlier than usual. My diary continued for that day:

> I went to work as usual. In the evening police cars toured the streets saying anyone who wished to be evacuated to the country could go to Hoy Street School and buses would take them immediately. Practically everybody from Old Canning Town went. We decided to evacuate ourselves to Blackmore the following day. That night Canning Town got it badly. Howard's wood yard and Worlands Wharf were well alight. We had to leave our shelters and go elsewhere as there was a danger of our house being caught on fire. We packed what we could in the Anderson shelter and left for Blackmore at 5am.

I remember that at that time we had a little black kitten, which I had placed inside my jacket. As we were chatting to the police just before leaving, one of them noticed the kitten, and said, 'Oh, what a dear little thing.' My father had no idea I was taking the kitten with me and exploded. 'You can't take that ....ing thing,' he said. 'Get rid of it!' and threw it down. I was upset, of course, but I was more upset at the distressed look on the face of the policeman who, when he had the opportunity, said 'I'm so sorry.'

To reach 'Benares' we walked through the night, to Stratford, with bomb damage everywhere, and fires still blazing. We eventually managed to board a Greenline coach to Brentwood, where we caught the usual single-decker bus to Hook End, and the plot. I described the following day, Tuesday, the

10th September in my diary:

> I wrote to my employers and told them I could not resume work owing to being evacuated. We heard that bus loads of people from Old Canning Town were being taken to Ongar, four miles away. Mum and I went there, in case we saw our neighbours. Fortunately we did and arrangements were made for Mrs. Fowler, Mrs. Rowe (her daughter) and the two children to be billeted with us. Mrs. Holding, our next door neighbour, Harry, George and Frankie, had a little bungalow in the field opposite.

So once again, 'Benares' was to serve a very useful purpose. Mrs. Fowler from number four, and the Rowes from number two took over the caravan, we had the shed, and the Holdings were close by.

Unfortunately, when the neighbours arrived, they brought with them some dreadful news. While they had assembled at Hoy Street School to await the arrival of buses to take them to Ongar, other people from Canning Town had assembled at South Hallsville School, in Agate Street close by. There were already several hundred people sheltering in the school whose homes had been destroyed. They were all awaiting evacuation, but the coaches did not arrive and at a quarter to four in the morning, the school received a direct hit. All were killed. Whole families were wiped out. Our neighbours could talk of nothing else and said that over three hundred people had been killed. Official sources put the figure at seventy-six, as this was the number of bodies recovered but very few people believe this lower figure. Local people believe there was a huge 'cover up' to conceal the enormity of the tragedy. It took fifty years for the authorities to commemorate the disaster properly, when in 1990 a memorial rose garden and a plaque was unveiled by the Queen Mother.

The raids on London continued into November. Occasionally there would be short trips back to Wharf Street to recover some cherished item. We were delighted when Mrs Holding, Martha, from number eight, collected our chiming wall clock. It had become part of her life as well as ours. The dividing walls were so thin, they could sometimes hear the clock ticking. She was pleased to look after it for us. It looked more appropriate in her cottage than in our shed.

We could have been happy at 'Benares', away from the London blitz, if only we'd had some money to live on. I did potato lifting for three days and on the fourth day could not straighten my back. To gather the potatoes, I had an apron made of sacking tied round my waist, and bent double, went along the rows of potatoes, picking them up and putting them in the apron. I then tipped them into a sack, then repeated the performance. We were

All dressed up for the pub outing. Uncle Bill, in top hat on left. Gran, with sausages, on right

paid three pence per sackful. At the end of the day I had earned four shillings. I am afraid I had to concede defeat after the third day. I was amazed at the skill and agility of the older villagers, who made no fuss at all and looked forward to the opportunity of earning a little extra money.

Soon after we arrived at 'Benares', my father returned to West Ham, where he worked at an A.R.P. post. The war had provided him with his first paid employment for many a year. He expected my mother to return as well, and when she preferred not to, he withheld maintenance. There was no work available locally, so mother and Marie rented a furnished room in Chelmsford and found work there. I remained at 'Benares' and later my maternal grandmother came to escape the blitz. She had only been with us for a few weeks when she had to return, as her husband, 'Uncle Bill' was seriously ill. Gran and 'Uncle Bill' were still licensed victuallers and ran 'The Lads of the Village,' in Kensal Road, just off Ladbroke Grove. Although he was ill, he tried to keep going and must have suffered dreadfully those last few days. On arriving back home at the end of October, 1940, grandmother contacted my mother in Chelmsford and she left for London immediately. I was still at 'Benares' and had hoped to join her at 'The Lads' shortly, but then I received the following letter from her. It was written the day after she arrived, on October 31st, 1940. I reproduce it here, as it describes so well the harrowing situation in London at that time:

> This is Thursday afternoon and I am writing to you and Marie to let you know that I am safe after a nightmare journey here on Wednesday night.
>
> I left Chelmsford about seven o'clock and got as far as Brentwood. From there I changed, with a wait of half an hour to Romford. In Romford I couldn't pick up a connection anywhere, but after about three quarters of an hour I got a bus (two-penny ride) to Chadwell Heath, to change again and go on to Ilford. I began to find out that all this inconvenience was due to the air raid, which I experienced when everything started going off round me on my ride to Chadwell Heath. It was ten o'clock when I reached Ilford and I was lucky enough to get a bus that was going to Aldgate. I thought I was landed, but my troubles had only just started, the further into London I went, the worse the bombs and guns were, but the driver kept on and I was thankful. When I got to the tube, there were no more trains to Westbourne Park. I got advice that the nearest I could go would be Paddington. Getting to Paddington was just awful. I never want to experience it again. I changed three times and each time I had to walk through tunnels and platforms of thousands of people, sleeping and sweating, and stinking of sweaty feet, (all half undressed) sheltering from the raids. They were even perched up asleep on the stairs and on the escalator banisters. When I did reach Paddington, the air raid was awful outside and I had to go back again and wait and the station master told me that Royal Oak had been bombed. I was frantic; not one of the taxi men would move because of the danger, but a decent porter tried hard for me and eventually I got a taxi, which put me down at Gran's. You can guess. No answer. I heard voices of guards at the bus garage and they were most kind to me. They knew where I belonged and made arrangements to make me comfortable for the rest of the night. It was now gone twelve. One of them tried for me again and got an answer at Gran's. Mr. Howley was sleeping there so I was taken home and slept on the tap room floor and saw mother at 5 o'clock this morning.
>
> Episode Two – Poor Uncle Bill, was took ill with pains on Wednesday morning. He wouldn't give in but Gran made him see a doctor. He was taken to hospital for an x-ray but was immediately operated on and had a lot of his inside took away. Had he lived, he would have suffered terribly and would have had a lot of inconvenience, but although he came too, and said it was awful, he just collapsed and

passed away, thirty-six hours afterwards on Monday morning at 5 o'clock. Well, Ivy, I wanted you to come here for a night, but I don't now. In the first place, it is too dangerous. I want to get back as soon as I can. I am afraid, then again, you wouldn't be comfortable. I would much rather you stay where you are. You see, we have got to sleep in somebody else's private shelter and they are squeezing me in; another one would make it look as though I was coming it. Ivy, it isn't worth coming up here, believe me. I realize now what a lot Hook End must have meant to me, when I felt so safe down there, even without a shelter. Uncle Bill is being buried at quarter to twelve on Monday morning. I shall be going home just as soon as I can after it is over to go to work Tuesday morning. I am going to write a few lines to Marie now, no, not pages like this and then prepare for an evening in the bar, but don't be envious of me. I am not looking forward to it a bit and when the alert goes, it will just be RUN. That is all now. Kindest regards to all at 'Benares'. With lots of love. Your Mum. PS Keep this for Marie to read on Sunday. I hope she will be over. I am asking her.

This letter is now nearly sixty years old. I came across it recently and didn't realize I had kept it. She did ask me to destroy the letter after Marie had read it, as she was afraid my father would find out where she was. I am glad I didn't.

Relations between my parents did not improve. He threatened dire consequences if we did not return, such as setting fire to 'Benares' one dark night, or blowing the place up. My mother took him seriously. These were very difficult and sad times. Our neighbours found other billets and Gran had remained in London, and that left me. So I joined mum and Marie in Chelmsford and looked for work there.

So our Shangri-La was to be short-lived. I think my father resented my mother's initiative, and the fact that she had a 'bolt hole'. The family was now scattered with the three youngest evacuated and Lawrie in the Forces. There seemed no prospect of any more carefree days on the plot. I think my mother's immediate problems clouded her judgement. The plot had become a source of friction, and being short of money anyway, she sold it, lock, stock and barrel, for less than she had paid for it. I tried to find it fifty years later, but expensive looking houses were all I could see. She should certainly not have sold it.

Meanwhile, back in Wharf Street the story unfolded. Father had sold all the furniture. (What a good thing Martha Holding had the clock.) Jimmy was fourteen in the December and had reached the statutory school-leaving age, so father collected him from Somerset and put him to work. He soon

Jimmy, just 14 yrs, with Johnny Ross, outside the Durham Arms, Wharf Street. Note the railway signal, which possibly saved the writer's life (see following pages)

became ill again and with nobody to look after him, my mother reluctantly returned home, but Marie and I remained in Chelmsford. Fortunately the air raids had eased off.

After Christmas, Marie returned and she and mother worked in Finzie's restaurant in Leadenhall Street. This was soon to be bombed and the restaurant closed. Although they lost their jobs, the good thing was that mother was able to purchase, very cheaply, chairs and other household items, and gradually restored 6, Wharf Street to some semblance of normality.

Not for long. Jimmy was soon in hospital at Worthing and Lawrie was in hospital at St. Albans having sustained a fractured jaw in a boxing match. He was never to match the skill of his father, or Uncle Harry, in the boxing ring, and neither did Jimmy, although both tried. Eddie didn't even try. The fractured jaw was further complicated when erysipelas set in. Lawrie had already had embarkation leave, and became separated from his unit for the second time when it went abroad.

I, too, returned home at the end of February and went to the labour exchange the next day. I secured a job and was about to embark on another chapter in my life. Just three weeks later, the present chapter of my life ended with a bang.

I was living at home, alone with my father, as the previous week Mum and Marie had been offered work at Eddie's nursery school at Bishops Stortford. It was residential, but they accepted it as it was a good opportunity to keep in touch with Eddie. I didn't really mind as my father was out most of the time and I was working. I ran the house quite efficiently and once I was organized it was easy to keep clean and tidy. To my surprise I found an attractive new counterpane in the bedroom cupboard and spread it out on my bed. I did not feel lonely, as many of the neighbours who had left London at the beginning of the blitz had now returned, including the

Holdings, next door. Martha, by the way, had had the foresight to leave the hall clock with Uncle Fred. That evening, 19th March, I was on my own. Lawrie was actually home on a few days' sick leave, and was out with friends. Although the 'alert' had sounded, we didn't usually take to the Anderson shelter until things got a bit noisy. I settled in for a quiet night and started to wash my hair, when Lawrie came rushing in and said I had left the light on upstairs and not drawn the blackout curtains. He hurried upstairs to discover that it was an incendiary bomb that had come through the bedroom roof and landed right in the middle of the bed, and right through the new bedspread which my mother had secreted away, for a special occasion, no doubt. Catastrophe!

We had been warned about incendiary bombs. These usually preceded high explosives and were used to guide the bombers on to their target. We had been told to keep a bucket of sand ready, to smother the bomb I believe, and a bucket of water. We all swung into action. Mr. Holding, Sam Rowe from number two, and Lawrie were to man the stirrup pump and pass buckets of water, whilst I was at the kitchen tap filling the buckets. This was the only tap in the house, the same tap that was the scene of our frantic morning washing ritual. The sand didn't seem to be required, so I tipped that out and filled the bucket with water. Very soon I heard a shout from Mr. Holding, 'Sod it! There's sand in the water and it's clogging up the stirrup pump!' He was a very mild mannered man and that was the strongest expletive I had ever heard him utter. Martha was different. She had quite a lurid vocabulary and one which would have made a 'trooper' blush. They finished up climbing the stairs and throwing buckets, bowls and saucepans of water on to the fire, abandoning the stirrup pump in disgust.

After that, Lawrie went out with friends to the Liverpool Arms, I think, in Barking Road. I again tried to wash my hair, when the raid became more intense. The Holdings called me to join them, saying I should not be alone. We might have gone to the Anderson shelter, but Lawrie came in again, shouting, 'Take cover! There's a landmine drifting on a parachute coming our way.' He had been on his way home, coming along Stephenson Street, and passed Mr. Brown standing by his gate. He bade him goodnight, and made some remark about the air raid, when they saw the land mine coming. I'm not sure where Lawrie went when he arrived home, but I dived with the Holdings under their table. Just in time. With a loud shattering noise, the house shook and the walls caved in. It was quite dark, so I had to feel my way around. Strangely, although I knew the walls were damaged, I still put my hands out, like a blind person feeling for a familiar spot, and was surprised when the hall wall, or passage as we called it, wasn't there.

After we picked ourselves up, we all went to the communal brick-built air raid shelter, at the junction of Bidder Street and Stephenson Street, where in happier times there used to be an annual fair, and before that a group of houses and a blacksmith's. It was a hazardous journey, through falling shrapnel, explosions close by and fires blazing all around. Our neighbours from Stephenson Street were already there, including the Ross family, who lived next door to the Browns, and also the two adult Brown sisters. Their gardens were too small for Anderson shelters, so they always used the public shelter, and just as well they did, as we were to discover the following morning. But before the night was over, several dramas were taking place.

Throughout the night, we could hear the noise of bombs dropping and sirens wailing. Occasionally somebody from outside would call in, asking for volunteers to fight fires, or attend to casualties. Mr. Holding looked as if he might go, but Martha was in a state of collapse. 'Don't leave me, Harry,' she pleaded. One neighbour in the next toilet to me, where we had gone to empty our bladders, called out in a state of panic, 'I can't stop! I can't stop!' Her husband was trying to pacify her. I thought, 'Silly woman. Of course she can stop, when her bladder's empty.' What I now realize is that she probably had an uncontrollable bowel movement, which under the circumstances would not be surprising. Lil Brown kept asking, 'Have you seen dad?' They all wanted to know what had happened outside. Lawrie had seen Mr. Brown, but that was before the land mine had exploded.

When we emerged from the shelter the next morning, we were able to discover the extent of the damage. The parachute carrying the land mine had been caught up in the railway signal, almost opposite Mr. Brown's house and visible from Wharf Street. Had it not been for this, the land mine would have exploded in Wharf Street. Unfortunately for Mr. Brown, his house and the adjacent houses received a direct hit. We were lucky to escape with our lives but many of our neighbours were not so fortunate. The whole block of houses was brought down and twelve people were killed, including eight from the related Peel and Bell families. They spanned several generations. Mr. Brown was missing for a few days, when parts of him were discovered up the big tree at the end of our garden. Several friends remarked, 'What a good thing Mrs. Brown was not there, or she might have suffered the same fate.' In fact she had died of a heart attack a few years previously. Two passers by were also killed. It took days for the rubble to be cleared and the bodies recovered. I was there when the two beautiful girls from the Bell family were discovered. I shudder when I think of it now. They were unclothed and inextricably entwined, and their bodies had the appearance of purple and white marble. Everybody in the house was killed, including the girls' mother and their aunt, Florence, or 'Flo', Peel. She was well known locally as she ran a mail order club, and called at members' houses for their weekly subscriptions. When picking up bits and pieces from our garden, I came across a wedding photo of the family and was happy to pass it on to some workmates of Flo's, when they came round seeking information. Mr. Bell, who was out at the time, was the only survivor. It had a devastating effect on him from which, I understand, he did not fully recover.

As soon as we could, we started to clear what remained of our houses. The 'Antediluvian Order of Buffaloes' lay shattered beneath the debris. There was no water, or gas, so we could not make a cup of tea. I looked a mess as plaster and dust had soaked into my wet hair. I found a lavatory cistern with some water still in it, so I retrieved that and had a wash. I then went into work and apologised for being late. 'I've just been bombed,' I said. I must have been in a state of shock.

My father contacted Mother and Marie in Bishops Stortford, and they came home immediately, and didn't actually go back. Poor Eddie. Just a brief glimpse of his mother and sister and they were gone. In the meantime, I had made neat piles of our possessions, such as they were. We had a box hanging on the outside wall, under a shelter, which held our medical supplies, our medicine chest, as it were. The contents were scattered all over the garden, so I collected what I could and placed them back in the 'chest'. When my mother looked inside, she said, 'These things are not in the right place.' I was amazed at her insensitivity. Was she in a state of shock, too, perhaps? When she managed to find her way upstairs, she went into my bedroom and was horrified. 'What's that bedspread doing out?' she said. 'It's ruined. If you hadn't got it out it would have been saved.' Up to then I had idolized my mother. She could do no wrong, but I think it was from then that I gradually had opinions that were different from hers. I suppose I was growing up.

That week, as we had nowhere else to go, we stayed in the public shelter in the basement of the Imperial Cinema, at the junction of Barking Road and Silvertown Way. We slept in bunks placed against the wall in tiers. A large Caribbean gentleman was housed in the bunk immediately above me. As far as I remember, he was the only non-white person there, so he was the subject of some comment. 'He's quite nice,' someone remarked. 'Have you noticed? He is ever so clean.' As if this was a matter of some surprise! I went to work every day from there, until my mother found a house to rent in St. George's Road, Forest Gate.

Throughout my time in Wharf Street, there had been neighbourly disputes, rivalries and some backbiting, but in the end, when the houses were demolished and the community about to break up, we became much closer than we had been hitherto, and we all helped each other. Not everybody was sad to see the houses go. They should have been improved or demolished years before, but not in the way we had just experienced. During the next few days I heard one of the rare political comments to reach my ears during my childhood in Canning Town. 'That's all they were fit for' said some of the neighbours. Mr. Burley, Ethel's father, went round with a hammer, breaking anything that was left unscathed – the toilet, the sink, even the 'kitchener' stove. 'I'll make sure the bastards don't put these together again,' he said. They never did.

A factory now stands on the site of 6, Wharf Street. The Durham Arms is still there, but no prying eyes look out for courting couples. The big tree is no longer there. I wish it were. Although it sadly reminds me of Mr. Brown, it was a relic of West Ham's distant past.

– 5 –

The TB Clinic

When I had left 'Benares' and joined Mum and Marie in Chelmsford, in November 1940, I was interviewed for a job at Crompton Parkinson's, the light bulb manufacturers. They were already working there, as cooks in the works canteen. I was successful and placed on a waiting list. In the meantime I worked as a shop assistant at Woolworth's. After a few weeks I commenced work at Crompton Parkinson's as a clerk in the 'fractioning' dept. This department was concerned with wire, the very thin wire such as is found in light bulbs and other electrical equipment. The width of the wire was precisely defined to several decimal points of accuracy, hence the 'fractioning' department. When Mum and Marie returned to West Ham just before Christmas, I moved in with Mr. and Mrs. Gurton, in Bishops Road, the couple from whom we had been renting the bed-sitter. They knew nothing of our problems and treated me like a much-cherished daughter. I had never been so well looked after. Their twelve-year-old son had been evacuated to Canada, and they missed him dreadfully. When he returned after five years, he had grown out of all recognition. They also had a very attractive daughter, in her twenties, who was very much infatuated with a major, and didn't spend much time at home, so I was the fortunate recipient of their warmth and affection. Mr. Gurton was a very hard-working coalman. Back in London, the intensity of raids had diminished and people were beginning to return. I missed the company of my friends, so I too returned, at the end of February. My foray into the world of wire of infinitesimal widths was as incomplete as my experience of screws and bolts had been.

As soon as I arrived home, George Fowler from next door greeted me with the information that he had arranged an interview for me, as a clerk, at a cable manufacturer's in Silvertown. He had written on my behalf, assuming he was being helpful. Neither the job, nor the location, appealed to me, so although I was grateful for his interest, I did not attend the interview. I did not therefore make the progression from light-bulb wire to cables. The next day I went to the Youth Employment Office, and was given a very professional interview. 'Do you want to work with figures, animals, or people?' I was asked. 'People,' I said. 'I'd like to work in a hospital.' As chance would have it, a vacancy was about to be created at the

Tuberculosis Dispensary, in Balaam Street, Plaistow. At that time, a new set up, the Civil Defence Medical Services, was being established in West Ham and an administrative assistant was required to work for the Medical Officer for Civil Defence. A very able and competent woman in her early forties was then Clerk to the Tuberculosis Officer for West Ham, and she was seconded to the new post, thus leaving a vacancy at the Dispensary. I was inexperienced, with very moderate shorthand and typing speeds and no substitute really for the capable Miss Bush. However, I went for the interview straight away and managed to take down a letter and type it. I secured the job, subject to a medical examination.

The next day I presented myself at the waiting room for my 'medical'. The formidable Sister Egerton showed me into a side room and said, 'Strip to the waist,' emphasising the word 'strip', which was the only word which registered. I wasn't having any of that so I did not remove my lavender-coloured satin french knickers, hand-made with scalloped shell edging. Just as well. When I heard the command, 'Enter', I walked into the examination room. I had by now developed a firm and ample bust. Dr. Galpin gasped in amazement. 'Oh, Miss Hicks! Do put something round you.' Apparently I should have retained all my lower garments and covered my top with a blanket. He called Sister Egerton, who provided me with a blanket. I got the job. I returned home and when I said where I'd been and where I would be working, my father said, 'Capital! Job for life.'

I commenced work on the 24th February 1941, just three weeks before the land mine destroyed our home, and the appointment was ratified at the next meeting of the Hospital Committee. Nearly sixty years later, I read a copy of these minutes, which stated that:

> The Medical Officer of Health reported that Miss Bush, clerk at the Tuberculosis Dispensary had been seconded for whole-time Civil Defence duties, and that in consequence thereof Miss I Hicks, 6 Wharf Street, E.16, aged 16 and a half years had been appointed as a temporary junior clerk at the appropriate scale of wages.

Well, I didn't know I was temporary. I stayed there for five and a half years, and the 'appropriate scale of wages' commenced at 19/5d per week. Out of this, I paid 15/0d to my mother and with the remainder had to buy my clothes and anything else I required. It was generally understood then, that as soon as children went to work, they paid for their keep and contributed to the family income, even at the age of fourteen, when boys, incidentally, also went into long trousers. During the first week, I was asked whether I wished to be paid a salary or a wage. When I asked what the difference was, I was told that a wage was paid weekly, and a salary was paid monthly. In each case, it was paid in arrears. As I could not hold out for a month, I opted to be paid a wage, and this was brought to me every week, by special messenger, from the Borough Treasurer's Office.

The Dispensary was housed in two pre-fabricated 'nissen-hut' type of buildings, erected, I understood, as a temporary measure during the First World War. Prior to 1912, dispensaries were charitable institutions; outpatients were 'dispensed' a variety of cheap, or free, unscientifically proven medications. They were thus in a position to continue to live at home and to work while they were able. Dispensaries spread rapidly after 1909, and TB became a notifiable disease in 1912. Doctors received one shilling per notification. In 1914, dispensaries became the responsibility of the Local Authority. These, together with hospitals, became the main providers of diagnosis and support.

The West Ham Tuberculosis Dispensary was in Balaam Street, at the Barking Road end. The two huts were erected one behind the other, in a narrow space between the Municipal Baths and a large 'country' house. In earlier times, the rear hut had been in greater demand, when T.B. was much more prevalent, but over the years, until the onset of the Second World War, there had been a steady decline. The rear hut was then used only once a week, when Dr. Keats, the Assistant Medical Superintendent at Dagenham Sanatorium, held her outpatient session. The front hut faced on to Balaam Street and was divided simply into four – the main waiting room and the Sister and Nurses room in the front, and Dr. Galpin's room and the Office at the back. All rooms were interconnecting. Dr. Galpin had been the Tuberculosis Officer for many years. He was both responsible for overseeing tuberculosis care in West Ham and was also a practitioner. He was an ascetic type of man, who appeared to me, then, to be in his sixties. He cycled in from Essex every day, Claybury, I believe, in all weathers and wearing sandals. Sister Egerton said he would never start work until he had emptied his bowels, no matter how long it took. He was a great advocate of eating plenty of green vegetables, especially the dark, outside leaves of celery, to the chagrin of many a TB sufferer; some patients had hopes of a quick cure, possibly with surgical intervention, unrealistic though this was and to be told to eat the outside leaves of the celery plant, must have been very frustrating and depressing.

It was a very busy dispensary when I was there. For instance, the annual report on the health service for West Ham, in 1944, stated that 5,163 examinations were carried out. In an attempt to make it more user-friendly, and to avoid the stigma people felt at attending a TB establishment, it was renamed 'Chest Clinic', but nothing else changed. Seating arrangements in the main waiting room were primitive. There were three or four rows of hard wooden benches, and on busy sessions, they were crammed. Sister

Egerton, seated at her table, in the same room took details of patients. There was no privacy. Dr. Galpin's room was off this waiting area, via a changing cubicle.

The work at the Dispensary, or Clinic, as it came to be named, involved seeing patients referred by GP's, following up contacts of notified cases, supervision of patients, either to ascertain whether they were continuing the regime of life established at the Sanatorium or recommended by Dr. Galpin. The two nurses, Nurse Schwer and Nurse Burkett, tested sputum, which they never came to terms with and often retched as they carried out the weekly routine in a room in the rear hut. My heart bled for them, as I saw them removing sputum from a little pot, scraping it on to a slide and then subjecting it to a dye. They also made regular home visits. In 1944, they carried out 684 sputum tests and also made 6,790 home visits. These visits were to check on conditions and make recommendations, not all of which could be carried out. Many patients could not have a bed to themselves, let alone a bedroom. Wage earners, for economic reasons, stayed at work when they should have been resting, and good, 'healthy' food and a balanced diet was difficult to obtain in many homes.

Dr. Galpin also devoted one day each week to Artificial Pneumothorax refills, or A.P. refills, as they were called, or just 'refills'. This involved deliberately collapsing a patient's lung, with the object of resting it. The theory was that the lesion then stood a better chance of repair. The lung was collapsed by inserting a hollow needle through the chest wall between two ribs, into the pleural cavity. The end of the needle projecting from the chest was connected to a tube, attached to two bottles of anti-septic fluid. By raising one bottle, the fluid flowed into the lower bottle, driving out air, which then flowed into the chest cavity, thus causing the lung to collapse. I caught a glimpse of this procedure once. It seemed so macabre, with the patient sitting calmly with a tube poking out of the chest. They would then get up and go home, or even back to work, probably by bus. These refills were repeated every three to six weeks, often for a period of a year or more.

The office was reached by a side door, which faced on to the Baths. It was very small, about the size of a single bedroom. Facing the door, sat Mr. Rowe, the Clerk, behind a small table on which stood an old-fashioned pedestal-type telephone. To the left of the door and extending along the partition which divided the office from Sister's room, was a counter, behind which I sat for most of the day and did all the typing for the Clinic, including reports, records and letters to patients' GPs. There was a door to Dr. Galpin's room, where I took down letters in Gregg shorthand. Behind me was a sliding hatchway, such as may be found between a kitchen and dining room. Sometimes this would suddenly fly open with a command or a request from Sister Egerton. To the right of the door, in front of Mr. Rowe's desk, was a gas fire. He seemed to spend most of the day in front of this, facing the counter, or my little enclave, with both hands in his pockets, 'turning over his money' and staring into space. Sister Egerton came in one day and whispering fiercely said, 'Take your hands out of your pockets, man. You should be ashamed of yourself, with a young girl like Miss Hicks in the office.'

I was given a great deal of responsibility, which I was pleased to accept. Soon after I started, when I was still only sixteen, I had to assess the eligibility of patients for 'Extra Nourishment'. They would stand on one side of the counter, and I on the other, while I asked them sensitive details about family income, such as how much each member of the family earned and how much rent they paid. At first, each individual member of the family's income had to be taken into account. Some would say, 'I don't know how much he, or she, earns. I only know what they give me.' I reported this to Dr. Galpin, and the rules were later changed, which allowed for a contribution of fifteen shillings from each working adult. I then divided the total income, with a deduction for rent, by the number in the family, and hey presto, their meagre ration of milk, butter, eggs and cheese, would or would not be paid for. Patients thought 'extra' nourishment meant just that, and expected the grocer to supply it in addition to the ration, but this was not the case. Just the ration and no more would be paid for. Solution? Change the name. We called it 'Home Nourishment'. The ration then was two ounces of cheese, four ounces of margarine, two ounces of butter, one egg every two weeks, and three pints of milk a week, or sometimes two pints. So paying for this amount would not have changed their way of life substantially. In 1944, 42 patients were in receipt of home nourishment, out of a total of 850 definite cases of tuberculosis on the register.

There were no x-ray facilities at the Clinic. Patients were taken by taxi, once a week, to Whipps Cross Hospital. The taxi owner would collect the previous week's x-rays and bring them into the office. This arrangement worked well for years, and we built up a good working relationship with the taxi owner. Again, in 1944, there were 709 x-ray examinations.

When patients required institutional treatment, the only place available was Dagenham Sanatorium. County Councils became responsible for Sanatoria in 1921. Before that the more advanced cases of T.B. were admitted to Poor Law Infirmaries, where most of them died. Many patients did not seek institutional treatment until it was too late, so many families knew of somebody who had died in Dagenham Sanatorium. Some patients refused admission if a member of the family had already died there.

The treatment at Dagenham, as in most sanatoria, consisted first and foremost of fresh air, rest, good food and graduated exercise. Some chronic sufferers of TB returned time and time again, to be 'built up' and then returned to the unsatisfactory conditions which it was thought gave rise to the onset of the disease in the first place. Some patients for economic reasons stayed at work for far too long and, without the drugs which later became available, their prospects were bleak indeed. The smaller group of patients were those who, having had some outward manifestation of the disease, such as the coughing up of blood, had sought advice early. For these there was greater hope. Most patients felt that more should be done and were not happy to lie in bed, sometimes month after month, seemingly wasting away. Ideally they were not discharged until it was felt they could carry out a full day's work. There was plenty of opportunity to put this to the test at Dagenham. Once patients were allowed up for most of the day, they undertook 'graded' work. For most patients on outdoor work, there were three grades:

(1) Light work. For two hours in the morning.
(2) Heavier work such as digging for two hours in the morning.
(3) Same as work in grade 2, but the patients work both in the morning and in the afternoon.

The female patients were employed in domestic work, washing up, dusting, and cleaning lockers, and in addition some did light gardening. I wonder what the 'grades' were in the private sanatoria of the rich.

Some sanatoria had 'rounds' or walks as a test of endurance, starting on short walks of half a mile and finishing up with as much as ten. All these rituals helped to relieve the boredom of a prolonged stay away from one's home and family.

Some A.P. treatments were given at Dagenham, but in 1937, Dr. Mayberry, the Medical Superintendent, was doubtful of their value in all cases. He reported:

> The more limited the disease, the more successful the result is likely to be. As a large proportion of these cases do well with conservative treatment, it does not seem justifiable to attempt an induction before a reasonable period of observation. With few exceptions, the more advanced cases should not be subjected to this treatment without very serious consideration. Over a number of years we have had the opportunity of observing the end results in the more advanced type of case. They were far from encouraging compared with the results in those patients who received prolonged conservative treatment.'

However, this 'prolonged conservative treatment' was not understood, or welcomed, by some patients and when an opportunity for surgical intervention was offered, they gladly accepted. One operation, which was performed at that time, was the 'thoracoplasty'. The object of this was to permanently collapse the affected lung, in those cases where a temporary collapse, or A.P. was not possible. These patients were sent to the London Chest Hospital for the operation. To collapse the lung, several inches of the upper ten ribs on one side had to be removed. This caused the chest wall to fall in, thus forcing the lung to collapse. This collapse was permanent; therefore the patient functioned on one, hopefully healthy, lung. George Cook, writing in his memoirs, 'A Hackney Memory Chest', underwent the fearful 'thora'. It was carried out in three stages, by Mr. Price Thomas, an eminent Harley Street physician, and performed under a local anaesthetic. George remembered hearing the 'metallic bong' as a section of rib was deposited into a bowl. He was left with a scar eighteen inches long and had to wear a surgical brace to support his weakened side for many years. What a difference the discovery of penicillin and streptomycin made a few years later.

Dagenham Sanatorium was the only one West Ham had to offer and I vividly recall the sad case of Flora. She was a very attractive young woman in her early twenties, and a single mother at a time when this was frowned upon and the term not even invented. She still lived at home and her young daughter, aged about two at the time, was being brought up by Flora's mother, as her own daughter, and sister to Flora. When TB was diagnosed and admission to Dagenham was recommended, Flora's mother was distraught. 'Please, don't send Flora to Dagenham,' she pleaded. 'I've already had three daughters die there.' Sadly there was no alternative. When her condition did not improve, she was eventually admitted to Dagenham Sanatorium. We saw her lovely daughter from time to time, as she was kept under observation. She was usually singing and was dressed in yellow, so we called her 'Canary'. Flora was later considered to be a suitable case for the thoracoplasty, and was admitted to the London Chest Hospital. Whilst she was there, a bomb fell in Balaam Street, and little Canary was killed, and Flora's mother was seriously injured and lay unconscious for several weeks. Flora discharged herself from hospital to attend her daughter's funeral and to watch over her mother. This caused her condition to worsen. I dread to imagine Flora's mother's state of mind when she eventually regained consciousness. Flora's condition deteriorated and she was readmitted to Dagenham Sanatorium, where she died.

Another sad case was that of a patient who had TB throat and lungs. He had previously had a thriving electrical business, which he lost when he could carry on no longer. His wife left him for a more affluent partner and the children were put into care. He could not support himself or find accommodation because of his condition. Seeing no way out, he committed suicide. I always found him to be a very pleasant and intelligent person and thought at the time that had it not been for his desperate financial circumstances, he might have pulled through.

These and many other sad stories had a great effect on me and helped to change my outlook on life. Where previously I had had a smiling acceptance of things as they were, I now began to question the type of society in which we lived and thought that 'something must be done'.

The housing conditions in many parts of West Ham were such that an infectious patient could not be isolated and in large families several members succumbed to the disease. I recall assessing one patient's eligibility for 'home nourishment', and when I asked the mother how many children she had, she replied in staccato fashion, 'I've 'ad eleven. Buried six.' One of her sons later received his calling up papers, and when he had his medical exam, had to produce a sample of sputum. This turned out to be positive, so he was referred to the Clinic. He proved to be perfectly healthy. His brother had obligingly spat into the container for him. He didn't escape call up. I thought it was a pity. He should have been excused on compassionate grounds. I hope he survived the war.

Some elderly patients had to sign the home nourishment form with a cross. I taught one woman how to sign her name. It was 'Grover'. She would sometimes get carried away, and write, 'Groverover'.

All the staff at the clinic were very caring, including Mr. Rowe. As one patient lay dying at home, she longed for an ice-cream. It seems hard to imagine now, but there were none available during the war, and nobody in that area had refrigerators, so a home-made ice-cream was out of the question. Mr. Rowe phoned all the cinemas and other likely places, but to no avail. Another patient wanted a banana, but we knew we couldn't help there.

Dr. Galpin was a very kind, gentle and hard-working doctor. He was rather 'distant' however, and rarely indulged in small talk. I liked him. We were fellow cyclists. We both cycled into work every day. For me, this was quite hazardous on occasions. Although trams had been replaced by trolley-buses, some of the tramlines still remained. Sometimes my bicycle wheel would get caught in these now redundant tramlines. The strangest thing, however, to happen on my journey, led to my having to replace the bicycle. I was cycling along, in busy traffic, when my front fork suddenly snapped. The front wheel fell away, and I was left holding the handle bars. Amazingly, I just stepped neatly to one side, and carried my bicycle home. It had been left outside so many times in the rain that it must have succumbed to rust. Dr. Galpin was interested in my cycle trips and would often ask me where I'd been. He would then say, 'Well done, Miss Hicks.

Keep it up.' On 'D' Day, on the 6th June, 1944, most people were rejoicing. I must have made some remark about it, when he was dictating his letters to me, and he said, 'Let us not forget, Miss Hicks. Many will not return. It is a sad day for some.'

Sister Egerton, although appearing fearsome, was very capable, as well as caring. She often gave me good advice, whether or not I asked for it. If I was off colour, she could tell. She once gave me a jar of cod liver oil and malt, 'to put me right.' On one occasion I had four very stubborn abscesses on my calf. She dealt with them in two days. Every two hours the hatch would fly open and she would call me into her room, where she applied a hot poultice. She would fit this in as well as dealing with a very busy waiting room.

During the war clothing was rationed. This did not have much impact on me as money was in short supply, anyway. There were no 'ox-fam' shops to help us out. I had a very limited wardrobe, made worse by the fact that one cold evening, when I was at evening classes, my winter coat was stolen from the cloakroom. One day, the hatch flew open again and I was summoned to Sister Egerton's room. I stopped what I was doing and reported immediately. She had a parcel of clothing in front of her, and said, 'Put that on. It's just your size.' She showed me a magnificent green suit, with a bouclé and corduroy jacket and a bouclé skirt. I tried it on and it was perfect. She said, 'You look beautiful.' Apparently, a young girl, very well provided for, had died. She was not previously known to us, being a 'notified death'. Her mother had brought her wardrobe to the clinic for Sister Egerton to give to a needy person. She obviously thought I was needy and I suppose I was. Certainly with the wage I was earning, I could never have afforded such a good quality suit. It served me well for many years to come.

Both the nurses were very sensitive people. After home visits they would describe some of the appalling conditions they came across. They were upset, not only by what they had seen, but also by their feeling of helplessness, in not being able to bring about a change. I was invited to Nurse Schwer's flat in Leyton one weekend. She made me very welcome, but what I remember most about the visit was the fact that I slept with the bedroom window open. I didn't recall having previously been able to do that, probably because of noise, pollution, or security, or possibly because the window was 'stuck'. I really enjoyed the experience.

Other people I remember from my TB Clinic days were two handsome medical students. Scabies was very prevalent at the time and sufferers were treated at the rear of the Baths, and had to pass the office on their way to treatment. They had to stand naked in a bath and were sprayed with some substance. The medical students were conscientious objectors and they were assigned to carry out this treatment. I wanted to get to know them more, but I never had the opportunity.

During the five and a half years I was there, many changes took place. The end of the war was still four and a half years away when I commenced at the clinic. Thousands more civilians were to die in air raids and still greater numbers were to die in battlefields around the world. We were not always aware of the tragedies as they took place, and only in retrospect do I wonder how we coped. Certainly work at the clinic continued uninterrupted. Throughout my period there, I was known by my surname. I started as 'Miss Hicks' and I left as 'Miss Hicks'. I was always treated with respect and consideration but never once, as far as I can remember, was called 'Ivy'. As a staff we did not meet socially. I was the only one who lived locally and there was, of course, a generation gap. However, we all worked well together, and I admired their commitment.

Meanwhile I led a very active social life, was introduced to cultural pursuits and developed a political awareness. My thirst for knowledge was sharpened and I spent several years attending evening classes at the Municipal College at Stratford. Many of the classes took place in the air-raid shelter. At home there were many changes, too. The diary and memorabilia which I kept at the time have been very helpful in recalling those formative years.

– 6 –

Adolescence in War-time West Ham

My career at the TB clinic was providing a stability that was perhaps less evident in these war time years in my home and social life; though the instability and uncertainties at home must have been even more upsetting for Pat and Eddie. For them there was repeated evacuation, loss of school friends and a return home to an unfamiliar district and a fragmented family. Even while I was adjusting to my new work at the clinic I was bombed out of house and home. I had three subsequent addresses before we finally settled in Selsdon Road, Upton Park. It was easy to find accommodation then, as many people had left West Ham. One noticed an empty house, made a few enquiries, and if all was well, just moved in. There was certainly very little furniture to worry about.

As a family we were far from settled. Shortly after leaving Wharf Street, Lawrie returned to his unit, and at the beginning of May, Marie, who was eighteen in April 1941, joined the Women's Auxiliary Air Force. When she left she recalls going through London after a very heavy raid. The attack on London on the night of 10/11th May had been very severe. Fourteen hundred people are reputed to have been killed. She recalls seeing fires still burning around St. Paul's and wondered how it could possibly have survived. There were huge, twisted girders alongside it and many fires were still blazing. She had a very difficult time getting to Kingsway, where she had to report. She was posted to Edinburgh, the furthest away from home she had ever been. Jimmy at this time was in a convalescent home in Worthing. So, out of six children, only one remained at home, me.

Marie, aged 18 yrs, in the WAAF.

Mother, second from left, at first aid post.

Mother was now working as a nursing auxiliary at the first aid post at Samson Street, Plaistow. It was attached to the isolation hospital, or fever hospital, as we knew it. Pat had spent several weeks there when she was two years old suffering from scarlet fever. In those days when a case was notified, the bedding was collected, disinfected and then returned. Marie and I had walked to the hospital every day to enquire about her progress and were always told, 'She's comfortable'. Mother remained at the first aid post for several years and often worked night shifts during air raids.

Our first move was to a house at 41 St. George's Road, Forest Gate. It was certainly larger than the one in Canning Town. There were three rooms downstairs; the front room and middle room had connecting double doors, and the kitchen was at the back. Unlike Wharf Street, where the downstairs front room faced directly on to the pavement, this house had a tiny patch of earth at the front, which at one time had been enclosed by iron railings and a wrought iron gate. These had suffered the fate of most iron railings at that time. They were removed for the 'war effort' and turned into armaments. The house was run-down and dirty. The bath was discoloured and there was no hot water system. There was hardly any garden, just a small back yard. We had expected Forest Gate to be an improvement on Old Canning Town, but the condition of the house was a disappointment. Worst of all, it was ridden with bugs. We were afraid to unpack what personal belongings we had for fear of contamination. We waged war on the bugs and dirt and kept our eyes open for other accommodation. About two months later we saw somebody moving out of a house opposite, at number 120. We asked if

Lawrie and Ivy in garden at St. Georges Road, Forest Gate.

anybody was moving in. There didn't appear to be, so as they moved out, we moved in. That is how it was done then. One first moved in and then searched out the landlord, and paid rent and rates. It was a much better house, with a slightly larger garden. Incidentally, whilst we were living at No.41, we became friendly with the family next door, and I often played cards with a young man there. He was later called up and sent abroad. When next I met him, he was blind, and he recalled the happy times we had playing cards in his garden.

By the summer of 1941, when we were living in Forest Gate, Rene's family were living in an attractive detached house in Harold Road, Upton Park, having returned from Chulmleigh, in North Devon, so we saw each other frequently. We enjoyed many activities together and when part-time classes started up at the Municipal College in Romford Road, Stratford, we decided to go along. They were held on Saturday and Sunday mornings,

Irene Green and Ivy Hicks, Summer 1941.

evening classes having been suspended due to air raids. I was quite excited at the idea of going to a college. We both studied English and French. I would walk from St. George's Road, through West Ham Park to Romford Road, a much pleasanter walk than if I had gone from Canning Town. We also had occasional cycle rides to Wanstead Park and Epping Forest. On the way we would stop off at a coffee stall at the 'Wake Arms', for a cup of tea. There would always be a very long queue. I remember stirring my tea as I walked away from the counter, when the spoon suddenly sprang up and out. It was attached to a long line of inter-looping elastic bands, which was then fixed to the ceiling, or counter; I forget which.

Eddie at Bishops Stortford, 1941.

One day we cycled to Bishops Stortford to see Eddie, who was then five years old. The last time I had seen him was when I went to 'Benares' in September 1940, at the beginning of the blitz. I had borrowed a bicycle and cycled from Hook End, Blackmore to Bishops Stortford. I had no maps and there were no sign-posts then, 'to confuse the enemy' should an invasion take place. I didn't know where I was going as I wasn't familiar with the area and was quite relieved when I arrived. It was worse coming home as I had left it rather late and it was getting dark. Cycle lights had to be very dim, and shaded. There were no street lights or lights from houses due to the blackout. It was a nightmarish journey. In contrast my trip to Bishops Stortford with Rene was a straightforward, pleasant one, as we knew most of the route, having cycled in that direction many times. We took Eddie out for the day, which I clearly remember as I have a happy photo of him taken then.

That summer of '41, Mum and I visited Pat in Umberleigh. We met Mr. & Mrs. Boucher, the elderly couple who were looking after her. Pat, who was now eight years old, had settled in very well and was well known in the village. Mrs. Boucher did the laundry for the 'big house'. Pat would collect and deliver it and always return with a 'secret' bottle of cream. It was illegal to make cream during the war as milk was rationed, but country folk had ways of getting by. The cream was never mentioned by name. Pat earned pocket money by pumping water from a well to fill containers in the house. She walked everywhere, to school, to the little church in Warkleigh and to

Pat with Mr. Boucher and writer on horse.

local farms to collect other supplements to the ration. When we paid a visit fifty years later, Pat relived those days and remembered the footpaths she had trodden. Some were overgrown and blocked. I wrote to the local Ramblers Association, pointing out the existence and long-term use of these paths. They were pleased to receive such information, as it was helpful in their efforts to recover lost paths.

When the young evacuees first arrived in Umberleigh and Mrs. Boucher went to select a child, Mr. Boucher gave her instructions. 'I want nought but a maid,' he said, meaning that he wanted a little girl. They didn't have a bathroom or a bath and one of the first things Mr. Boucher did was to go out and buy a zinc bath for the 'little maid'. He went out on his horse and came back with a long, narrow, zinc bath, which he 'wore' on his head like an elongated helmet. On our recent visit, Pat and I saw a bath in the garden, covered in nettles and brambles. The present owner of the cottage confirmed that it was, in fact, the same bath. A very smart car is now locked in a garage, formerly the stable, which housed the horse. Pat was secure there, as London was still not a safe place to be.

At the end of 1941, there were Commando raids on the fjords of Norway. For some reason, my half-brother Jimmy, my father's first son by his first wife Charlotte, volunteered for the Commandos. We saw him from time to time as we did Charlotte. He was a very gentle, mild-mannered man, who had trained to be a tailor. He was in the Cheshire regiment and not at all the 'macho' type that I imagined would volunteer to join the

Commandos. He took part in the Vaagso raid on December 27th 1941, which was an early Commando operation. The object was to destroy German military installations. The Royal Navy bombarded German batteries prior to the attack by the Commandos, who then went in using landing craft. Resistance was fierce, but 'all objectives were achieved at a cost of nineteen killed', one of whom was kind and gentle Jimmy. Apparently one hundred German prisoners were brought back and some volunteers for the Norwegian Free Forces, but not Jimmy. He was thirty-one and left a wife and five-year-old son, who was born two days before my brother Eddie. He was buried at sea and his name is recorded on the Brookwood Memorial, Surrey. This memorial commemorates 3,500 men and women of the land forces who died in the 1939/45 war 'on service outside the main theatres of war' and who have no known grave. This includes men and women, such as Jimmy, who were members of raiding parties against Norway, St. Nazaire and Dieppe. He is also remembered in a memorial book in Chester Cathedral, dedicated to those in the Cheshire regiment who lost their lives during the war.

Incidentally, this half-brother Jimmy had another half-sister, named Joan. She was the daughter of Charlotte, who had remarried. Charlotte's relationship to us became known quite by chance. When Marie was about thirteen or fourteen, she was in the school hockey team when it had a match with another school. During the course of conversation with her opponent, the name 'Hicks' was mentioned. 'Oh,' said Joan. 'My mother was previously married to a 'Hicks' and I have a brother and two sisters with that name.' They seemed to be related somehow and reported back to their respective parents when they returned home. Shortly afterwards, my parents summoned Marie into our front room, with serious expressions on their faces. She thought she had committed some misdemeanour. It was then that they divulged the fact that 'Aunt Charlotte' was in fact my father's first wife and that Joan was her daughter by her second husband. I can't understand why there was a need for so much subterfuge. I became friendly with Joan in the '40's. We shared many interests and also some friends.

In the autumn of 1941, the Russell Old Students' Association was re-formed after a break at the beginning of the war. Dr. Morris, the Geography teacher at the Russell School, and the one who had given me such good advice prior to my first interview, had the inspiration to organize its resurrection. He lived in Terrace Road, which was near to the school in Queen's Road, Upton Park. Harold Road, where Rene now lived, was also close by. Had I still been living in Canning Town, I probably would not have been able to attend its many functions and I am sure my life would have taken a different course. I threw myself wholeheartedly into its many activities, which included a dramatic society, badminton, netball, Sunday

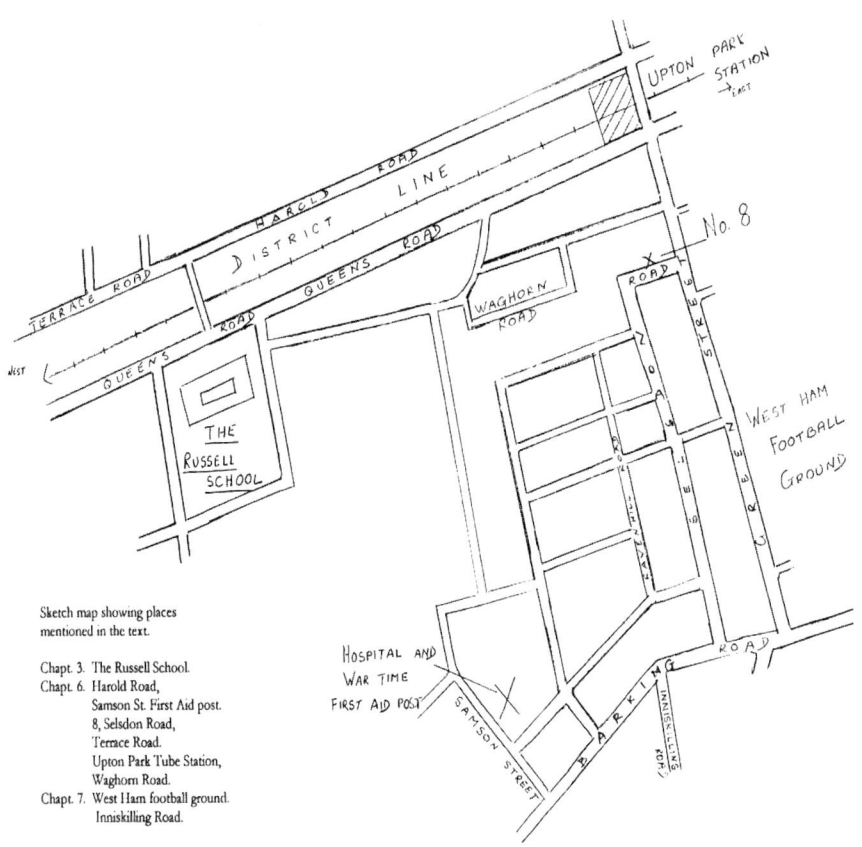

Sketch map showing places mentioned in the text.

Chapt. 3. The Russell School.
Chapt. 6. Harold Road,
   Samson St. First Aid post.
   8, Selsdon Road,
   Terrace Road.
   Upton Park Tube Station,
   Waghorn Road.
Chapt. 7. West Ham football ground.
   Inniskilling Road.

rambles and the very popular club night, on Fridays. I could walk to these from home.

'Life with father' seemed such an anti-climax after all these exhilarating activities. He wasn't getting any better, and I was beginning to doubt his sanity. Both parents were working irregular hours, including night work. He didn't take kindly to not finding my mother around whenever he was at home and there would be violent outbursts. At this time, the beginning of 1942, Jimmy was in Claybury Hospital. His hip was very painful and was slow to respond to treatment. There was just my mother and I to be at the receiving end of my father's outbursts. One day in March, he packed up his clothes and left, saying he would never return. We doubted this as he had done the same thing before. He always returned after a few days saying he was hungry and demanding to be fed. It had happened several times at Wharf Street. My mother suspected he was off to see a woman and hoped it would be permanent, but he always returned. For the few days he was away, we would celebrate. I associate one of the absences with 'haddock ears', or 'addockears', as it was pronounced then. In preparing a haddock fillet, the haddock is trimmed, the head, fins and tail are removed and a good portion of edible haddock comes away as well. This was sold very cheaply, as 'haddock ears'. On this occasion, the day my father left, my mother came home from Rathbone Street market with a huge parcel of this delicacy. When boiled, and with the bones and fins removed, the remaining flesh provided a tasty feast. When my father next left home, we said, 'Can we have 'addockears'? We couldn't always rely on haddock. Sometimes it was crabs claws. Obtaining the edible flesh took a little more skill, but it was great fun.

He did return then, of course, and during the spring of 1942, things were coming to a head. I saw no reason why I should suffer my father's tantrums. I was working and could support myself and so could my mother. One day, after my mother had made sandwiches for my father, he threw them at her, saying, 'What do you fucking call this?' I had up to then accepted my father's behaviour, as I assumed I had no alternative, but at seventeen, I was beginning to stand up for myself. I faced him. 'Don't you treat my mother like that,' I said. He went berserk. I was punched in the face, grabbed by the throat and pushed against the wall. My mother then tried to get between us. When he left to go to work, I said to my mother, 'I'm not putting up with this. You do what you want to. If you want to put up with it, that is up to you, but I don't see why I should have to. I'm leaving.' She pleaded, 'Don't leave me Ive.' So we both decided to leave.

The next day I went into work with a bruised face and a black eye. 'Good heavens, Miss Hicks!' said Mr. Rowe. 'What have you done?' I said I had been playing cricket with my cousin and the ball hit me in the eye. No more was said. The next Saturday I was alone in the office at the clinic, as Mr. Rowe and I worked alternate Saturdays. I plucked up courage and telephoned West Ham police station to report my father's violence. I was told to report in person as nothing could be done over the telephone. I didn't go of course, and in fact was quite relieved that no action was to be taken. I was reminded of the time when my mother actually did call at the police station. She had four children then and asked for help. She was told, 'You've been married for ten years and had four children and you've just discovered you can't stand him? Go home, Mrs. Hicks and try again. Have another child. That'll put things right.' She returned home and actually had two more. My father was fourteen years older than my mother, an attractive woman. He was unsteady on his legs and walked with the aid of a stick, 'due to the boxing', so those who weren't aware of the situation suspected my mother's motives.

However, on this occasion, my mother and I spent some time looking for somewhere to live and eventually found a flat nearby, at 45, Waghorn Road. It was in poor condition and we secretly spent two weeks getting it ready. On Tuesday 23rd May 1942, we prepared to leave, whilst he was at work. All the furniture was my mother's, as he had sold the last lot, but she was fair. We went through everything. 'One for him, one for us, one for him, one for us' – cutlery, crockery, everything. And then we moved to a secret address. When he returned from work, there was just a note. Wow! It didn't end there.

The next day when I went to work, I said to Mr. Rowe, 'I have to report a change of address.' 'Really, Miss Hicks,' he said. 'Why is that?' 'We've left my father,' I said. 'Oh, I see,' said Mr Rowe. No more was said. The following Sunday, whilst I was out rambling with the Russell Old Students, my father came round to Waghorn Road three times, each time carrying a case full of rubbish and deposited it in the porch way. Pinned to the door was a large notice, 'Two prostitutes live here. I have thrown them out and their rubbish.' I do not know how he discovered our whereabouts, but there must have been ways and means. So much for a fresh start.

A week later, we went to visit Jimmy in Claybury hospital. Whilst we were waiting for a bus at Stratford, we saw my father. He came up to us, shouting, 'These are two fucking prostitutes,' and other obscenities, and lashed out. A man came to our aid and my father gave him such a punch that he knocked him down. Just then a bus came along. They were only one an hour. In our confusion we jumped on the bus. I felt so guilty as the bus pulled away, leaving somebody who had come to our aid sprawled on the ground, but everything had happened so quickly, that there wasn't time to think.

Even that was not the final episode in the drama. During the war, when one lost any property due to enemy action, it was possible to claim some compensation. After we lost the home in 6, Wharf Street, my mother obtained the necessary forms and meticulously claimed for all items lost. As my father had sold the contents of the home whilst we were at 'Benares', there now wasn't much and what there was had been purchased by my mother. She was scrupulously honest and did not claim for the value of the articles, but what they had cost her. As everything was second hand, this did not amount to much. The sum total was £37. This was accepted by the local authority and when a cheque came through, it was made out to my father and sent to him at St. George's Road. He paid us a visit, and laughing, waved the cheque in my mother's face.

In July 1942, Eddie was six years old, and, by now, too old to remain at the nursery school. For some time my mother had been requested to make arrangements for him, but with all the domestic upheavals, this was difficult. He could not be kept at Bishops Stortford any longer, so he had to leave. Another wrench for Eddie. He was sent to Warkleigh, Umberleigh, where Pat was staying, but he knew nobody there. Pat said that one day at school the headmistress said to her, 'Come with me. I've got your young brother here.' She looked around and could see nobody she recognised. Eddie did not know Pat, either. They did not meet at school, and lived with different families.

We visited them both shortly afterwards to see how they were faring. Grandmother came as well. She was still living at Westbourne Park, but mother's brother Bert and wife Lala, were now running the 'Lads of the Village'. It had been offered to mother, but because of domestic strife, she felt unable to accept. So Bert and Lala left the home at Benares Road, Plumstead, and moved in with grandmother. Incidentally, grandfather William Homes had died on the 1st May 1934, much to my mother's great distress. She said that he had 'choked to death'. On his retirement, aged 70 years, he had himself fitted with new dentures. Being unfamiliar with these, he bit his tongue. This swelled up and so did his throat, to such an extent that he could not swallow. He died in hospital, unable to drink even a sip of water. When I obtained his death certificate many years later I discovered he had, in fact, died of TB lungs and laryngitis. Yet up to his retirement he was still working as a chef at the Mansion House, in London.

The journey to Devon was a tortuous one. We had planned to travel by the night train. As it was a bank holiday Waterloo station was packed and we queued up for two hours for a ticket. Gran was knocked down and trodden on, as well as the eggs she was taking to Devon. The ration then was two per month. She had ten and they were all smashed. Where did she get them from I wonder? My mother always described her as a 'good business woman.' We were pleased to see Pat and Eddie. We were happy with Pat's arrangements but Eddie was with a 'cold fish' of a woman and it didn't seem right. Brother and sister saw very little of each other and never did 'bond'. I think the hurt they suffered when they were separated from their family had a lasting traumatic effect on them.

Just before we left for Devon, brother Lawrie called on us. He had been living with my namesake, Aunt Ivy, and Uncle Curry, my father's youngest brother, having had a disagreement with my mother. He broke the news that he had been discharged from the army on health grounds. He hadn't really been well since the attack of spinal meningitis. Also he was to marry a young Welsh girl, whose sister was a friend of Curry and Ivy. Unfortunately we were unable to attend the wedding as we were just off to Devon. In fact, we were all to marry without either parent being present.

For some time Mum and I had been looking for somewhere better to live and an estate agent's clerk promised to bear us in mind should anything turn up. Eventually we were offered a newly redecorated house to rent, with a small garden, in Selsdon Road. It was near to Upton Park station and also close to the Russell school. We were both delighted. We moved on November 2nd 1942. This was my fourth address since Wharf Street.

I was beginning to enjoy life now. For a time, Rene and I went dancing on Saturday nights at the Hammersmith Palais and the Opera House, Covent Garden, and danced to the 'big bands' of the period. There was never any shortage of partners. There were also many local dances organized by groups, for fund-raising. Joining in with all the old students' activities, we met many more former school friends. We joined the Russell Old Students' dramatic society, which put on many successful plays. The first was a J.B. Priestley comedy, 'Mystery at Greenfingers', in November 1942. We always had large audiences and good write-ups in the Stratford Express, the local newspaper. They were usually performed at the Plaistow Little Theatre. I continued to perform in at least two plays every year until October 1946. As a group we would often see other performances, for instance Vivien Leigh in Doctor's Dilemma at the Haymarket, on 29th December '42. The County Borough of West Ham had a Youth Organizations Committee and put on sports championships, music festivals, and youth weeks, which the Russell Old Students joined in enthusiastically. We took part in everything with the exuberance of youth, netball, athletics, swimming, rambling, singing, verse-speaking, impromptu speeches, and even bible reading. We didn't want to miss a thing, as if there was no tomorrow, and sadly for some, there was no tomorrow.

As my activities increased, so did my circle of friends. New names appear in my diary. I am still in contact with many of them to this day.

Among those who took part in the plays, apart from Rene, were Fred (Ferdy) Waterson, Vera Hills, Stan Roope, Harry Lane, Bill Speedy, Jack Baker and many others, who I then counted among my circle of friends. It was through Ferdy that I became involved in another fulfilling chapter in my life. For some time he had been involved with the Bancroft Boys' Club in Prince Regent's Lane, Custom House. He ran a club there for local boys, which was very popular. The club was sponsored and supported by the Bancroft School, at Woodford Green. It had started off in Shipman Road School, but then a fine, purpose-made building was erected, with a gymnasium, showers, toilets, an office, canteen and a quiet room.

Early in 1943, some of the Russell old students were invited to a party there and again a month later for an old student, Bert Southcott, who was going into the Air Force. There were always parties, either for friends who were called up or who were on leave. Vera and I began to help with refreshments and gradually became very useful. Dances were organized on a regular basis to raise funds for the club. These were held at the Municipal College, Stratford. We became cloakroom attendants, ticket collectors and raffle organizers. Another helper was Jack Baker who lived a few minutes walk from me. Ferdy lived at Elm Park but had no trouble getting to Upton Park Station, on the District line, just a few minutes walk from Selsdon Road. He would often stay with Jack for the night and sometimes Vera would stay with me. Soon there was a 'foursome'. Either Jack or Ferdy would ring and we would all go out somewhere, either to a concert or to a dance. We would usually finish up at Selsdon Road, for a cup of tea and a chat. Perhaps Mum would be at work, but Jimmy would always be there. On my nineteenth birthday, Jack bought me an attractive necklace and matching brooch. He was a draughtsman, and one day showed me a plan of his ideal house. He became a regular visitor to Selsdon Road, on some pretext or other, or just for a chat. My mother liked him very much and would encourage him to call, especially as she usually found him some little job to do. She perhaps hoped I would take the relationship further. However, I was enjoying the company of all the group, or 'gang' as we called it and sharing an 'ideal home' with one in particular would have spoilt that comradeship. In any case, there was so much I wanted to do and becoming committed to one person was not yet my intention. Jack continued to help out at Bancroft for a while, but soon met a young girl at a party. Marriage and fatherhood soon followed.

The boys at the club were aged between twelve and fifteen. They were very responsive to anything that Ferdy organized for them. On Sunday mornings, Vera and I took them for hikes in Epping Forest and the Essex countryside. We also joined them on a camping holiday over the August Bank Holiday, 1943. There were seventeen boys there aged from ten to fifteen and Vera and I and Jack's father cooked for them all. During the day, Ferdy, Jack and Bill put them through strenuous physical activity, so they were always ready to eat. In spite of rationing they were well fed. It was not exactly 'cordon bleu' but my diary reveals such delicacies as soup and bread, rissoles, which I made, stewed apples and rice pudding, bread and meat paste, or lemon curd and jam, biscuits and beans. I do remember making a gigantic roly-poly pudding, which 'floored' everybody. They didn't move for several hours afterwards. We all returned home on Monday evening. Vera and I cycled back, Jack walked home with some of the boys and the trek cart and all the luggage, and Bill and Ferdy took the other boys home by bus. The trek cart was the usual way then of carrying equipment, so campsites could not be too far away. The Bancroft boys were fortunate in having a site available where they could camp, free of charge. Mr. W. C. French, a local builder in Essex and a former Bancroft school pupil, was also a farmer and he always made one of his fields available for the boys. We met up again in the evening at the club with other friends and it was back to work the next day. Every available minute was filled then. There seemed no time to spare.

As friends were called up, we kept in contact with them. Ferdy kept them in contact with each other by typing out news from each of them, duplicating the sheets and forwarding each one a copy. He kept this going throughout the war and amassed a vast amount of correspondence, which he has kept. Vera and I edited one issue of his 'Bancroft Mission Gazette' in January 1945. There were twelve names on it then – Gunner Arthur Stump, who was looking forward to the 'Grand Re-union Do', Bill Speedy in the Navy, who on his last leave stayed up with me till 2 a.m. stoning raisins for the Bancroft Christmas Cake. Nobody believed us! Pupil Pilot Bert Southcott was in Bloemspruit, South Africa, F/Sgt. Bob MacNish was in India, and so was A/C Harry Lane, at Dum-Dum. Tragically Harry was to die of beriberi a few months later. As Ferdy had the key to the club, it was no problem having farewell or re-union parties. The senior Bancroft boys enjoyed these as well. Arthur Stump had two brothers in the forces, and every time one came home on leave, his mother and sisters would invite us all round for a party. We usually stayed all night. For Arthur's twenty-first birthday party, there were fourteen of us for breakfast! They were a great family.

In August of 1943, the headmistress of the school in Umberleigh began to think about Pat's future. She was obviously an intelligent girl and would no doubt qualify for admission to a grammar school, but there were none in Umberleigh. The nearest was in Barnstaple, which would have meant her living there. As things were getting quieter in London, she suggested that Pat return, attend the local school, and go through the process of the 'eleven plus' examination. So, on the 5th August, Pat returned and Eddie came as well. Although Pat was unhappy when she first went to Umberleigh, she had settled and had eventually adjusted happily to the life. Now she was put through another unsettling experience. She had not returned to the area she had left and did not know the school and had no friends to return to. Selsdon Road and the area around Upton Park were in stark contrast to the country lanes and fields of Devon. No birds sang in Selsdon Road. Eddie, too, was unsettled once more. Little thought was given then to the harm that was being done to young children as they were constantly moved around. Pat did pass the 'eleven plus' and went to Plaistow Grammar School.

Both Pat and Eddie must have been particularly bewildered. Not only were Lawrie and Marie not at home, but neither was their father, of whom they had no unpleasant memories. In fact, my father adored Pat. There had been a six year gap between Jimmy's birth and Pat's, in spite of the fact that contraception was not the order of the day. I cannot explain that. I do know that when Pat arrived she was made a great fuss of by all the family and so was Eddie. They returned from evacuation to a different sort of household. In retrospect, I wish I had spent more time with them, but my life was pretty full anyway.

That autumn, evening classes recommenced at the Municipal College and I, together with Vera, decided to go along and follow a matriculation course. There were very few subjects on offer and the only ones available to us were English, Maths and French, Chemistry and Heat, Light and Sound. These last two subjects were quite foreign to us, but if that was all there was, then so be it. We went to classes for five evenings a week, and studied one subject each night. With homework to complete, our social activities were somewhat curtailed. We did manage to squeeze in the dramatic society, Sunday morning rambles with the Bancroft boys or Russell Old Students and the occasional party.

Although it may sometimes appear otherwise, life was not 'just a bowl of cherries'. The war and its ramifications had an impact on us all and was brought home ever more closely. Vera's brother who was in the Air Force did not return after a raid on Germany. My cousin Harry, son of Harry Homes, my mother's brother, was killed in North Africa in 1943. He was in the Grenadier Guards and just twenty-two years old when he was killed in Tunisia at the Battle of the Horseshoe, Mareth Line, on 17th March 1943. Captain Nigel Nicholson wrote an account of the battle in his book *The Grenadier Guards in the War of 1939-45*. Faulty Intelligence led to the men being forced to cross a minefield, so heavily mined that later 720 mines had to be lifted before the bodies of 69 Grenadiers could be recovered for burial. Not only was the area thought to be clear, but the Germans knew of the impending attack, as an officer, carrying the battle plans, had been captured. The 6th Battalion had never been in action before and as they set off, they understood they were about to attack a lightly held outpost! What a waste of young lives. In a letter from Harry's mother to the Commanding Officer, she wrote, 'I hope I am not taking up too much of your valuable time.' A year later, her son's property was forwarded to her. It consisted of a book, *The Fire of Life*, a belt and a pullover. Harry was the same age as his father's brother Fred, when he was killed at the Somme, but Fred's body was never recovered. Cousin Harry has a memorial grave in a Commonwealth War Cemetery at Sfax, in Tunisia. I have since visited the area where the battle took place and photographed Harry's headstone. It's in a dry, sandy plot, where flowers struggle to survive, but the 'keepers' of the cemetery were doing their best and were very helpful. They produced a book of remembrance to show us.

All this and more was leading us to have serious discussions about the world we lived in. I was beginning to acquire a general political awareness, though my own affiliation and loyalty to a particular party was yet to come.

Cousin Harry's grave at Sfax, Tunisia.

– 7 –

Moving On:
War Ends, and I Leave the Clinic

Although nationally the most significant event of 1944 was D-day, the 6th June, for those of us at home, life just carried on. We had our own ups and downs and our own crises. To my shame, in my book of 'jottings', I have only one line for that day, '6th June. The Allies invade Normandy. Hard fighting continues.' The next entry is for Sunday, 11th June. 'Vera and I again took the Bancroft boys hiking. There were thirteen of us. Spent Sunday evening at Bancroft.'

Most of my entries at the end of '43 and throughout '44 then related to Saturdays and Sundays, as during the week, Vera and I were fully occupied grappling with the intricacies of chemical formulae and heat and light. We never did get round to 'sound'. There was plenty of it around, however. Air raids disrupted our lessons occasionally, and although we experienced the noise made by falling bombs, we never had the time to analyse this scientifically. On Friday, 26th November '43, at a Russell club night, we heard a bomb drop too close for comfort. The following day we discovered that it had in fact dropped in Inniskilling Road, Plaistow, quite close to Selsdon Road, killing fourteen people. Intermittent raids continued and in fact on January 21st, a 'little blitz' on London commenced and on Saturday 29th, a dance Jack had organized was a failure owing to a heavy air raid at the time. Raids gradually began to ease off, and although we did not know it at the time, Tuesday 18th April 1944, saw the last air raid on London, by conventional planes, that is.

D-day had raised people's hopes. Perhaps the end of the war really was in sight. There was a more relaxed atmosphere, and then something disastrous happened. Just a week after D-day, a strange 'aeroplane' flew over. It was not a German bomber or fighter that we had come to recognise. It had a monotonous drone and kept a straight course, regardless of what was aimed at it. Then the drone stopped, the plane fell, and blew up, or so it seemed. My diary states, 'Raids on S.E. England and London, by Germany's 'secret weapon', the pilotless aeroplane. There have been several air raid alerts and bombs have fallen close by and caused considerable damage.' These 'flying bombs' posed a considerable threat. They seemed unstoppable and came by day and night. The characteristic drone, followed by silence, was unnerving. One could hear and see them flying over. There was nothing one could do except to hope that it would not cut out over one's head. Schoolchildren were evacuated again. Nearly one and a half million people left London before the end of July. Pat and Eddie went to Lawrie and Glenys, at Rochford, Essex for a few weeks. At the end of September Pat was again evacuated, but this time with the Plaistow Grammar School, to Corton, near Lowestoft. Vera and I saw her off from Liverpool Street Station. Eddie stayed with Lawrie. Throughout the period of the flying bombs, over six thousand people, mostly Londoners, were killed. A total of 58 'flying bombs' were dropped on West Ham alone.

Although our activities were often disrupted, we tried to lead as normal a life as possible. In fact, our interests were taking us beyond West Ham, Epping Forest, and Essex. In the spring of 1944, Ferdy had begun to speak of Rose Weaver, a woman in her thirties, with whom he worked. She was a socialist and they held long discussions every day. We already had an informal discussion group at the Russell Old Students' club nights, on Fridays. While activities such as table tennis and various board games were taking place in the hall, a small group of us would gather at the far end of the stage and discuss a wide range of subjects. In West Ham there was no shortage of subjects that needed to be discussed, such as poverty, unemployment, housing, health, post-war development and so on. Dr. Morris would be at the centre of these discussions. I wonder what our former school head teacher, Charles Truelove, would have said if he had known what was taking place on his hallowed school stage, where he had daily pontificated with such an air of infallibility. I first joined in when I heard the question of Epping Forest being discussed. Dr. Morris was keen to prevent the encroachment of the Forest by housing developments. 'People from West Ham need a breathing space, a 'lung' to escape from pollution and cramped conditions,' he said. I expressed the conventional point of view as I did for some time. 'If people had decent houses,' I said, 'they wouldn't need to escape. There is plenty of room on the edge of Epping Forest.' I was the perfect fodder for a discussion group with radical opinions. My husband and I are now life members of the 'Friends of Epping Forest.' Our discussions were enlivened by Ferdy's contributions after his discussions with Rose Weaver. Before long, five of us, Ferdy, Vera, Stan Roope, Harry Lane and myself, were invited to Rose's for tea, and discussions, of course.

This 'mind stretching' activity was accompanied by several 'firsts' for me. On Sunday, 16th April, all five of us went to an orchestral concert at the 'Orpheum', Golders Green. The programme included Beethoven's 5th Piano Concerto, the 'Emperor'. The soloist was Solomon. I had never before seen so many musicians in one place. We did not have television then, so it was a completely new experience for me. I was surprised that so many musicians could work so well together. I was impressed by the atmosphere as much as the music. I continued to enjoy orchestral concerts, in particular the Harold Holt Sunday concerts, held at the Albert Hall. On the 21st January 1945, Ferdy, Vera, Stan Roope, sisters Marie and Pat, and the Bancroft boys went to a concert by the London Philharmonic Orchestra. Shulamith Shafir was the soloist for Greig's Piano Concerto in A minor. We went again with the Bancroft boys in March when the conductor was Pouishnoff and the soloist was Dorothy Pouishnoff, and again in April when Cyril Smith was the soloist. The Bancroft boys were beginning to appreciate classical music as well and when we listened to records at the club on Sunday evenings, they too came in, 'provided they were quiet.'

In July '44, I had another new experience. Rose Weaver, Vera and I had a two weeks walking holiday in North Wales. Harry Lane who was on embarkation leave joined us for the first few days and Ferdy joined us later. I had no experience of climbing, and no suitable footwear, yet we decided to climb Snowdon. The walk up was slow and tedious, as we ascended by the railway track. Half way up it seemed to be raining, but we carried on. Suddenly the rain stopped and we were walking in bright sunshine. We had actually walked through a cloud. The sky above had always been a mystery to me, as it is to children, and here I was, looking down on to the clouds for the first time. I was nearly twenty years old and had only just risen above the clouds!

A few days previously we had gone to Caernarvon to see Harry off, and not having a camera, we decided to have a studio photo taken before he went. I'm glad we did, as we did not see him again. He was posted to Dum Dum in India, where the station seems to have been particularly badly managed. As mentioned in the previous chapter, he died of beriberi, a disease which is entirely preventable. It is caused by a deficiency of vitamin B and is suffered by people who live mainly on grain that has had the husk and germ removed, such as 'polished' rice. When I looked into his service record at the Public Record Office at Kew, I discovered that there was in fact a great deal of sickness among the air crews at the station. There were constant complaints of a 'shortage of crew due to sickness'. Twelve months previously Harry was a fit young man, climbing mountains in the Lake District. Now he was dead. Vera and I called on his mother, a widow, when we heard the sad news that she had lost her only son.

After the holiday, we travelled home by train, which was delayed and arrived at Euston in the early hours of the morning. We then had to wait several hours for the tube station to open. We travelled thence to Upton Park, Selsdon Road, and breakfast. There we found a note from Vera's

With Rose Weaver, standing, and Harry and Vera. July 1944

mother to the effect that their home had been destroyed by a 'doodle-bug', as we were now calling the 'pilotless aeroplanes'. We, too, had suffered some bomb damage and were now sharing our Anderson shelter with Lizzy and Lil Brown, friends from our Canning Town days.

Doodlebugs continued to fall until the end of August '44. At the end of July one dropped on a trolley bus at Dames Road, on the edge of Wanstead Flats, reportedly killing sixty people. Another dropped on the bus garage at Greengate Street, Plaistow, and this blasted Vera's new home in Barking Road. On the 2nd August one dropped on the West Ham football ground, so close to us that we also suffered some more damage. Actually, just eight weeks previously, the football ground had been used to assemble D-day embarkation troops. The ground was surrounded by a high brick wall and high gates, presumably to prevent eager fans from getting in without paying. On this occasion it served to stop soldiers from getting out. One soldier, who was there, married Rene four years later. He stated, many years later, when my husband and I met them both, that the morale amongst some of the troops was pretty low. They had seen active service in North Africa and now expected a break and did not take kindly to being thrown into another campaign. Some were trying to go AWOL, so tanks and lorries were put up against the gates to keep them in. My future husband was also in West Ham football stadium, in June '44, on his way to Normandy.

Incidentally Rene joined the A.T.S. at the end of 1944. With my busy life at evening classes and at the Bancroft boys club, we had not seen so much of each other and the last dramatic production that we were in together was in June 1944.

Gradually, an effective strategy was devised to deal with the doodlebugs. Apparently they moved no faster than an ordinary aeroplane and could be shot down. So instead of waiting until they reached London, anti-aircraft guns were moved to the coast and by August, eighty per cent were being destroyed.

With people now talking about the end of the war, I began to think about my future. I was expecting to sit the matriculation examination in January 1945, and was gaining in confidence. In my ignorance, I imagined that success in the exam would be a tremendous step forward and I applied to University College Hospital for training in radiography. I was interviewed and offered the post of trainee radiographer, but I was unable to accept this offer, as I would have had to work for nothing. I was then offered training as a darkroom technician, with a salary attached, but I did not relish spending my working life in the dark. To my shame, I replied to an advert for a job as secretary to Dr. Henderson, a Harley Street Radiologist, and was interviewed and offered the job, at a salary much greater than I was receiving at the clinic. However, I was still bound by the 'essential works order', and the Ministry of Labour would not release me from my post at the clinic. I was disappointed at first, but upon reflection, I am glad I did not enter the world of private medicine and privilege.

Once the flying bombs were dealt with so effectively, we thought we were safe, particularly as the Allies were having success in France. In fact, on 7th September, Duncan Sandys announced, 'The Battle of London is over.' If only! The following day we were faced with a new threat. We now know that on that day the first rockets were launched on London. On 16th September, I noted that 'an unidentified missile dropped up the road and blasted a great many houses and shops.' These were more destructive than the flying bombs and came without warning and there was no defence against them. Apparently plans were made to evacuate London. Eventually, 11,015 rockets were dropped killing nearly three thousand people, before their launching sites were overrun by the advancing Allied armies. 27 were dropped on West Ham.

Before the war West Ham had a population of approximately a quarter of a million, but the Medical Officer of Health's report for 1944 stated that it had then decreased to half that number. He also stated that, 'When we reached the second half of 1944, West Ham was again meeting the full brunt of aerial attacks by flying bombs and rockets.' However, except for a short period when Bancroft club nights were cancelled due to the danger of flying bombs, we managed to enjoy life. Many of our friends were now in the forces and at Christmas I had greetings from Harry in India, Arthur in Holland, Bert Crooks in Alexandria, Bill Speedy 'at sea', Bert Southcott in South Africa and George Fowler, our next door neighbour from Wharf Street, then in the Middle East.

In January 1945 Vera and I sat for the matriculation examination. Unlike today's GCE's, the matriculation subjects could not be taken individually, with a failure in one subject meaning just that. All five subjects had to be passed, 'en bloc'. A failure in one subject meant a failure to matriculate. However, as a wartime concession, it could be passed, or failed, in two separate parts. On this occasion, we each passed in one part and failed in the other. We continued to attend classes and were both successful in June 1945. I thought the world was now 'my oyster'. I went to the Youth Employment Office to break the good news and in effect said, 'What can you offer me?' I had in mind a Lady Almoner's post, or advice on the necessary qualifications I would require. I left with the impression that matriculation wasn't such a big deal. It was the bottom rung of a tall ladder. I had a superannuated local government job and that was the best I could expect. They were right, of course. However, I enjoyed the experience of evening classes, especially meeting fellow students and lecturers for

From Bert Crooks, near Alexandria

From Arthur in Holland

From Harry

From George Fowler in the Middle East

a cup of tea and a chat after lectures. There were always 'discussions'. Wartime conditions had given rise to a great deal of thought, even amongst the Forces, I understand. When I was asked what I would sign up for next, I asked, 'What is there?' The maths lecturer said, 'Why don't you do Inter?' When I enquired what that was, it was explained that it was an 'intermediate' qualification for admission to university. It could be studied without following a full degree course. I didn't see how I could go to university anyway, as I had to earn a living, but I thought I would like to continue studying. So in September 1945, I started classes in Economics, History and Geography.

I had since the Spring of 1944 been to many political meetings and became interested in a very small political party known as the Socialist Party of Great Britain, a grand name for a party with only a thousand members. We made frequent visits to Hyde Park on Sundays to listen to the speakers there. A very popular speaker, and member of the SPGB, was one Tony Turner, who spoke to massive crowds every Sunday. When he died in 1992, Ian Aitken wrote about him in the 'Guardian', on the 26th February:

> It wont mean much to anyone under 50, but Tony Turner is dead. His death marks the departure of one of the last great practitioners of the Hyde Park, Tower Hill and Lincoln's Inn Fields school of open-air oratory, on a par with Donald Soper. In the forties and fifties Turner was the star turn of a cuddly little organization grandly named the Socialist Party of Great Britain. Its approach was Marxist but it believed there could be no real change until enough people had seen the light. It was Tony's job to show them the light and he blinded them daily with the brilliance of his wit. His technique, though simple, demanded an IQ of near-genius level. He would serve up 15 or 20 minutes of glorious knock-about humour, in which hecklers were crucial. Once he had drawn a large enough crowd from neighbouring meetings he would sock the socialism to his audience for five minutes or so. I don't know how many converts he made – my guess is quite a lot. . . . With such a star in its firmament, it is odd that this little party didn't prosper. But it still survives to this day, and for Tony's sake, I retain a warm affection for it.'

We didn't regard it then as a 'cuddly little party'. It was very active and ran classes in economics, public speaking and writing and all branches held outdoor meetings. After the Hyde Park Corner meetings we would go to the Lyons Corner House 'salad bowl', where we could eat as much as we liked for two shillings and sixpence (twelve and a half pence). There was a vast range of various meats, fish, cheese and desserts on offer. I thought this was the nearest thing to socialism one could get – 'from each according to his ability, to each according to his needs.' In April 1945, we went to a debate at the Shoreditch Town Hall, on 'Socialism or Capitalism', between Clifford Groves for the SPGB, and Sir Waldron Smithers, MP for Orpington. This was arranged by the Hackney branch. The hall was packed to overflowing with an estimated 1,500 people present. Smithers was not very convincing and when Groves said, 'If you want a monument to capitalism, look around you,' we knew what he meant.

The members of the SPGB held the view that the Party was small as nobody was admitted who did not understand 'the socialist case'. To achieve socialism, people must understand it, and want it. It could not be imposed from above, by a minority of 'believers' on to a majority who did not understand its implications. The democratic nature of the Party appealed to me. In April 1945, Stan Roope, Ferdy, Vera and I, presented ourselves to the West Ham branch, held at a school in Manor Park. There, the branch of about sixty members questioned us to ascertain if we really did know about socialism. Ferdy was asked, 'What is socialism? Did he believe in God? Why did he choose the SPGB?' Stan was asked, 'Why did you not choose the Communist Party?' Vera and I were also 'grilled'. Vera was asked what she understood by the 'class struggle' and I was asked why the SPGB insisted upon democracy within the Party. After satisfying the branch, we were duly admitted. As one branch member said later, 'We thought the revolution was just round the corner. We had never had so many join in one day.' Most of the members were people of integrity, very well read, and had a genuine social conscience. Not expecting ever to get a majority of members in parliament in their lifetime, nobody aspired to political office, and were therefore not tempted to 'sell their soul to the devil.' Some of its members I met then are among my closest friends today.

The end of the war in Europe was now in sight, just three weeks away in fact. On Monday 7th May, Churchill announced that the following day would be regarded as the end of the war in Europe, VE day, as it became known, and that Tuesday and Wednesday would be public holidays. The Japanese were yet to be defeated, and VJ day was yet to come. There was great excitement, of course, although the end of the war had been expected for some weeks. That evening many people lit fires in the streets, and sang and danced. Some of us from Russell walked round, surveying the scene and eventually finished up at Prince Regents Lane, Custom House and met many boys and their families from the Bancroft club. Somebody produced a piano, and Ferdy was encouraged to play. He played all the old familiar songs and we sang well into the night. Everybody seemed happy but as we walked home, we were in fact rather sombre, as we reflected on the awfulness of war, the loss of life and the misery that still remained for some. We rather doubted that all that should be done would be done. Not even in our wildest dreams could we have imagined the havoc that would be wreaked by the dropping of two atomic bombs, three months later.

I had to work at the clinic the next day and in the afternoon we listened to the radio at 3 p.m. to Churchill's speech. After it was over, Sister Egerton wept and Dr.Galpin prayed. There were no words between us and I just carried on typing. I had not expected the end of the war to be like that.

During the war there had been a coalition government, so there had been no elections, but now there was to be a general election on July 5th, my mother's 44th birthday, in fact. The SPGB put up a candidate in the North Paddington constituency without any expectation of success. It was regarded as an opportunity to hold meetings and distribute literature. On most evenings and weekends for many weeks I helped out at the committee rooms in Harrow Road. I delivered leaflets, stuck up posters and did door-to-door canvassing. At least I thought I was doing something. The result was not announced until the 26th July to allow time for servicemen to vote. 472 people voted for the SPGB candidate, but we were not dismayed. We were encouraged to think that after only a few weeks campaigning we had converted 472 people to Socialism! It was worth the effort, we thought. The Labour Party, however, was elected with an overwhelming majority and it was thought that the servicemen's votes contributed largely to this.

Clement Attlee replaced Winston Churchill as Prime Minister. There was again rejoicing in the streets, as there was on VE day. However lives were still being lost in the war against Japan and it was not until two atomic bombs were dropped, one on Hiroshima on the 6th August, and one on Nagasaki on the 9th, that the Japanese surrendered unconditionally on the 14th. The 15th was declared a national holiday, and VJ day. I do not recall any great excitement, such as that which followed VE day, as it was more or less expected, but those families who still had men in South East Asia must have been very relieved. Most people, however, were now more concerned with thinking about the future, myself included.

As men and women gradually returned from the Services it was obvious that vast numbers required education and training for peacetime occupations. Many people's education had been curtailed or interrupted owing to the war and they now wished to take up where they had left off. Others had become conscious of their lack of education due to their wartime experience. To remedy this, the government introduced the Further Education and Training scheme, or F.E.T.S., as it became known. Anyone who could prove that his or her education had been interrupted owing to the war could apply for a maintenance grant to attend full-time education. There was also a great shortage of teachers and the 'Emergency Teacher

Training' scheme was introduced. This provided a one-year intensive residential training course for people of 21 years or over. The minimum qualification for acceptance was matriculation, or, failing that, a satisfactory performance in writing an essay. Ferd, Vera, Stan and I decided to apply for this course and were all accepted, except Vera, who, not yet being 21 years, had to follow the traditional two year course.

I had heard about the F.E.T.S. from fellow students at evening classes and assumed it was essentially an ex-service person's grant, but was encouraged to apply. Could I prove that my education had been interrupted because of the war? Certainly on paper it would appear so. The reality was somewhat different. Before leaving school in 1940, I had been offered the opportunity of transferring to a grammar school, but with the future being so uncertain, and the fact that I had had 'two extra years' already, I was unable to accept. Financially it was impossible anyway. Had it not been for the blitz I might have become immersed in the production and sale of screws and bolts at 'Essenbee Products, Ltd.' In my favour I could prove continuing effort to remedy the disruption in my education 'caused by the war'. Had I not gone to evening classes to matriculate and commenced an Intermediate B.Sc. (Econ) course? My work at the TB clinic prevented me from entering one of the services. To my great delight, my application was successful and I was awarded a maintenance grant to enter University, dependent of course, on getting a place. This was fantastic. It was like suddenly coming into a fortune. However, it meant I had to spend a year to qualify for university entrance and then three years at university for a degree and then another year for the teaching qualification. I was already 21 years old. I would also have to go on a waiting list and would not be likely to enter university until I was 23 years old. The emergency teacher-training scheme seemed attractive. In just one year I could be earning money. Waiting lists were long and we all wanted to get started, so I decided to go for whatever came up first.

Whilst we waited for admission to various colleges, we continued with our Russell and Bancroft activities and visits to theatres and orchestral concerts. In the summer of 1945, Ferdy, Vera and her sister Doreen, and I, had a walking holiday in the Lake District. My last holiday with Ferdy and Vera was in the summer of 1946. On that occasion we caught a train to Derby and made a cycle tour of the Pennines and returned via the Lake District.

I had an interesting experience in November 1945. Dr. Rich, an old Bancroftian, and a helper at the club, had often participated in our discussions at the club and knew somebody at the BBC who ran a programme called, 'To start you talking'. He asked if I would be interested in taking part in a discussion on the problems of sex. There would be an impromptu discussion first with a large group, from which a script for a small number would be produced. I thought I would go along. I was given a letter for Dr. Galpin requesting a day's leave of absence, and stating that the BBC would reimburse me for loss of pay. The discussion was entitled, 'Why should sex be a problem?' Upon reflection I am amused at how I came to speak with such authority. For me, personally, sex had not been a problem. I just avoided it. I had been brought up to believe that this was what all men wanted. 'Don't trust 'em. You'll get trapped. They ruin your life,' and similar dire warnings had been heaped upon me. Alongside this was the fact that most of my friends were males. During the war we had formed a comradely, fraternal, supportive group and 'pairing off' would have spoilt this, even had there been the opportunity. I was quite happy as things were. However, I did know that many of the women in Canning Town were 'trapped' through economic circumstances. They married perhaps whilst already pregnant in order to support themselves and the child and stayed in the relationship for the same reason. With my mother's experience in mind I suggested in the discussion that women should get to know the man intimately before embarking on marriage, both temperamentally and sexually. I was selected by the producer, Christine Dudley, for the scripted presentation. My view was probably rather a radical point of view to be expressed on the BBC in those days. I must have given the impression that I was a 'free spirit', and available to gain experience in a relationship, for one of the men in the discussion group attached himself to me. He was very persistent, and travelled all the way with me from Broadcasting House to Upton Park station and then to Selsdon Road, where I bade him farewell and shut the door. I wonder if this discussion is still in the BBC archives. I'd like to hear what I committed myself to, on that day in 1945.

By the summer of 1946, I had still not obtained a place for the one-year teacher's course, so I pressed on with evening classes for university entrance requirement. I was in any case keen to learn how government worked and the part economics and history played in shaping the society in which I was living. I continued to work at the TB clinic and although sufferers from TB still presented a distressing picture, we were more optimistic about the future. Apart from a sharp increase in notifications from the outset of the war until 1942, there had been a steady decline since then and with the discovery of penicillin and streptomycin, there was hope perhaps of a 'breakthrough'.

The shortage of teachers and college places turned out to be not such a disadvantage after all. The London County Council was desperate for teachers and in their search for likely candidates scanned the teacher training waiting lists. So it came about that one day that summer I received an invitation to attend an interview for a post as an uncertificated teacher, whilst waiting for admission to a training college. It occurred to me that if the LCC had such a scheme, perhaps West Ham would have one also. I contacted the education office and was called for interview. They were furious with the LCC for 'poaching' one of their likely candidates, and one who had received all her education at the expense of the County Borough of West Ham. They offered me a teaching post, to commence in September 1946.

So it came about that my five and a half very formative years at the TB clinic were coming to an end. I was very sorry in a way. I had learned a great deal there and the staff had been very kind to me, and seen me through some very difficult years. The clinic had been the one stable feature in at times a somewhat precarious existence. I left with their blessing, and very warm, sincere best wishes from Sister Egerton, who had always encouraged me to 'move on'.

I left the clinic on a Friday at the beginning of September, 1946 and a few days later was teaching at the Ashburton Senior Girls School, Custom House.

– 8 –

Three Mills School, Stratford

At the beginning of September 1946, I reported to the headmistress of the Ashburton Senior Girls School, Custom House, and was given my timetable. It consisted entirely of physical education, without a break. I'd had no training and was given no instruction; but what proved to be the greatest shortcoming, however, was the absence of a whistle! All I knew about teaching was what I had myself experienced. On the positive side, I had youth and enthusiasm, and at the beginning of the week at any rate, physical fitness. I found most of the girls to be rebellious and undisciplined. This was not surprising given the unsettling effects of five years of war, with evacuation, bombing, and general 'loosening of reins', followed by a shortage of teachers and inadequate school buildings. Classes were large, approximately forty girls in each. The only place available for physical exercise was the school hall, which was surrounded by classrooms. Fortunately there were two netball courts which I used as often as I could. This occupied only twenty-eight girls – four teams of seven – but when taking into account those without plimsolls, or otherwise appropriate clothing, and those with headaches and sick notes, this number was manageable. A whistle would have helped considerably. I could produce a whistle by inserting four fingers into my mouth and curling my tongue backwards, but this was difficult to do 'on the trot'. I tried to buy a whistle but was unsuccessful, and was too exhausted after school to spend too much time trying. My throat became evermore painful as the week progressed.

 Each afternoon as we played netball, I noticed a young woman with a small child watching us from the road which ran alongside the netball courts. Towards the end of the week we made contact. 'I thought it was you,' she said. It was Maud, a fellow evacuee, with whom I had shared a bed and bath at Mrs. Norton's in Chelmsford. She and I had then gone on to the Lakins and shared a bed with Jean Lakin, much to Jean's discomfort. Maud lived nearby and suggested we meet one lunchtime, or after school. She said she could get me a whistle. By Friday, I had lost my voice completely, so after school I caught a bus and went to the education office at The Grove, Stratford. I said that I objected to teaching nothing but physical education. I did not mind teaching this for part of the week, but I also wanted experience in classroom teaching. The education officer agreed and told me not to report to Ashburton the following Monday, but to go to Carpenters Road Junior and Infants School instead. I was pleased about this, but unfortunately, I lost touch with Maud.

At Carpenters Road, I was again thrown in at the deep end. I had a class of infants and had to collect their dinner money and fill in the attendance register, as well as keeping them occupied. I really did not know what I was doing, but the staff were sympathetic. Apparently, as long as I was still on my feet at the end of the day and hadn't harmed anybody, I was doing well.

Most of the teachers were older women, except one, who was the same age as me, and she entered the staff room like a breath of fresh air. She had been teaching for three years, having unusually started at the age of nineteen. As a wartime concession she was able to start the two-year training course a few weeks before her eighteenth birthday. She was a very competent teacher and I admired the way she was prepared to take on the rest of the staff and to challenge their somewhat cynical attitude towards teaching. She came from Norfolk, where her father was the stationmaster at Martham and until she came to Stratford to teach, she knew nobody there. She was a member of the Fabian Society and I took her along to some of the S.P.G.B. meetings. Before long, after 'passing the test', she became a member. After six weeks, the teacher who I had temporarily replaced returned and I was sent to the neighbouring Three Mills School.

Three Mills school in Abbey Lane was opened in 1895 with places for 1,576 pupils. It had a primary department on the ground floor and a senior school above. It was similar in design to many other schools of the period. For two weeks I taught in the junior department in a room with desks rising in steps. There was no room for the children to move about and it must have been very unpleasant for them sitting in a desk for hours on end. I then went upstairs to the senior school. There was a large rectangular hall in the centre of the building, with classrooms leading off and a staircase at each end. In the centre of one of the long sides was a dais reached by a few steps on which stood the headmistress's desk, rather like a throne. When she had the time, which seemed to me to be quite often, she would sit at the desk and survey the scene. All the classrooms were to the front of her and to the left and right. Mine was on her left. On her desk was the signing-in book, which all teachers had to complete on arrival. I was given a first year class, the lowest stream of about three, I think, and requested to do the best I could. In effect, I was given a free hand and I don't remember having a timetable except for those occasions when we swapped classes for boys to do woodwork and the girls to do needlework and likewise for netball and football. I think we 'doubled up' for music.

The class was not too large, about twenty-three. The children were aged eleven to twelve and came from that unfortunate group of children who were five at the outbreak of war and should then have started school. In the book, 'War over West Ham', by Doreen Idle, written in 1943 and prepared for the Fabian Society and Ethical Union, she stated:

> 'Those children who should have started schooling at five, and instead started at six or seven, are the most affected. In one school of between three and four hundred children, there was not a child of seven who could read . . . concentration is said to be poor in elementary schools. It seems that small children are more easily unsettled in this way than older ones. There is also a greater coming and going through evacuation than among older children.'

This was written in 1943 and it was this group of children who then went on to suffer the unsettling effect of doodlebugs and rockets in 1944 and early 1945. Although, for many of the children in my class at Three Mills, their performance was below standard, they were by no means of low intelligence. For a variety of reasons, they had missed out. Some, even, might now be diagnosed as dyslexic and given preferential treatment. They'd had a raw deal and should have been compensated for their educational deprivation, but were instead placed under the care of an inexperienced, uncertificated teacher. They were lively and enthusiastic and gave me a warm and friendly reception. I did not expect to enter college until the autumn, so I felt it was incumbent upon me to do the best job I possibly could. Actually, far from being at a disadvantage, I was in a very favourable position. To begin with, I understood these children. I had come from the same background. They lived in the 'single cold tap' type of house that I had been brought up in, in Wharf Street, and the Bidder Street school which I attended would not have even featured in a 'league table' of desirable schools. My own brother Eddie was just two years younger than these children and I knew how unsettled he was. Also I was young and healthy, and not restricted to the confines of a syllabus.

The desks were arranged in rows, in pairs, and there was very little space between the rows. My desk was raised on a small plinth, designed it would seem to distance the teacher from the pupils. There was a shortage of materials, especially paper, so there was little opportunity for children to develop their artistic or literary potential. It 'used up too much paper'. I had learned from Dolly Dowling that children had to be kept occupied, so I purchased odd rolls of cheap wall paper and ceiling paper, and cut it into squares and this was freely available at all times. I also made sure there were plenty of coloured pencils available. They loved this and produced some interesting drawings, not always executed in silence. One, Billy Gormer, would draw airplanes and bombs and make the sound of planes crashing and bombs dropping as he did so, as though drawings should have a sound track. Pictures were pinned on the wall, and the classroom became 'alive'.

I made a pillar-box for the classroom, where pupils could post letters to me on any subject. This proved to be very useful and encouraged them to try their hand at writing, instead of the copying they had been used to. For many of them this was a struggle, but they were uninhibited and really made an effort.

One of my responsibilities was the school netball team. If we had an away match, I had to leave the class and set them work to do. They hated this, as usually a senior boy had to supervise them. One letter read, 'Are you going to put a prefect when you go out. Do not put a boy on us please.' On the other hand, when we had a home match, they could watch and the ups and downs of the fortunes of the netball team featured largely in their letters.

P.T., or Physical Training as it was then called, took place in the hall and I usually changed into shorts for this and encouraged them to do so as well. This caused great excitement, as the letters proved. Charlie wrote, 'All the boys sed are you going to were your p t cloce plece.' And from Hilda, 'When we have drill, will you put your drilling clos on and some of the girls will put on our dilling close. love from Hilda.' There were many letters like this. By presenting them here as they appeared, I do not think I am doing them a disservice, as I have had letters from them since, and they wrote beautifully. I had letters requesting tracing paper and more spelling tests. The pence table was in great demand, probably because they and their parents could appreciate its usefulness. I can still repeat it, singsong fashion, rising in multiples of ten and twelve. 'Twelve pence are one shilling, twenty pence are one and eight pence, twenty-four pence are two shillings. Thirty pence are two and sixpence,' and so on, culminating in, 'hundred and twenty pence are ten shillings,' which we said slowly and decisively, emphasising the 'ten'. They loved it. I think I did, too. I had desperate pleas to 'write out the pence table for me,' and one letter said, 'Someone has took my pence table out of my desk and I do not know them properly.' So the pence table even drove one of them to theft. A box of pen-nibs went missing from my desk and I must have kicked up a fuss, as there were many letters on the pen-nibs saga. Some expressed sorrow, some divulged names, but best of all, from Roy and Dennis, 'Dear Miss Hick. I am sorry we took a nips.'

During the lunch break for a few days a week, I taught ballroom dancing in the hall. I think they enjoyed listening to the records as much as anything. This was a great success and some of the older boys from other classes joined in, sceptically at first. I still have a beautifully written letter from

> Three Mills school,
> Stratford,
> 11-3-47.
>
> Dear Miss Hicks
> I am sorry the three boy had take the pen nips. Miss Hicks wear do you think I will come with the test. Well it is all I can say so cheero for now
>
> Bolttp.
>
> form Gladys and Hidd
> xxxxxx

Light Fingers

> 7-3-47
>
> Dear Miss
> I hope you will get this note I am santen yo. I kent not go twon yor esye and get any pen nopes
>
> from fred

> Dear miss
> some once has tock my pencetabel out of my Desk and I do not know them properley
>
> from Charle to miss

> Dear misshick
> I am very sorry we took a nips
>
> Roy and Denn
> Dennis

Presents

Three Mills School
Stratford E 15
1.3.47.

Dear Miss Hicks thank you for your letter I wish you would tell us what you would like for your present wold you like a pair of stokings would you let me know

from
Marie

Dear miss
this sweet is good
for a cold
but it is
vere strong

from
Charlie

Dear Miss Hicks
Could you write down my pense tables and I on going to buy you four pencils for a present.

Roy Morgeason

Three Mills
School

Dear Miss Hicks, the class and I are going to buy you a going away present we do not know wote to by you so I hame askin you wot uou wald licke. We can not get to miche muney to geuer but we are trying to to get an nufe to buys a smale present for you

yors sisley
Peter Andrew

> Three Mills school
> Stratford E.15
> №. 28-2-47
>
> Dear Miss Hicks
> I do not wont you to leave becoses you are a nice teacher. agan.
> But will you by back Pleases Miss Hicks will you learn me to dance.
> from Phyllis hopping
> you will oblige me
> P.S I will be at school all this week.

Dancing

> A. Flewitt
> to Mr Davies
> Three Mills School
> Stratford

> Dear Miss Hicks.
> I am writing to you, to express my gratitude for the dancing lessons you have gave me, and also for some of my friends, who did not like dancing at first but now jump at the chance of going dancing now.
> yours sincerely
> A Flewitt

> Dear Miss Hicks
> Thank you for your dancing lessons and you are very sporting teacher
> An Unknown Visitor

A. R. Flewitt from Mr. Davies' class, which reads:

> I am writing to you to express my gratitude for the danceing classes you have gave me and also for some of my friends, who did not like danceing at first but now jump at the chance of going danceing now. Yours sincerly.

It was letters like this that kept me going.

Sometimes I would get little presents, such as the cough sweet I received, accompanied by, 'This is a bit hot and good for a cold.' I had a promise of drawing pins, and four pencils. In February, there must have been some suggestion that I was leaving at Easter, and there was a flood of desperate letters. I didn't actually leave until the summer, when they moved up a class any way. Typical was the letter from Peter Andrew. I hope he doesn't mind my reporting it as it was written, as I know he writes perfectly, now:

> The class and I are gowing to bye you a gowing away present. We do not now wot to by you so I hame arskin you wot youe wald lick. We can not get to miche muney to gever but we are trying to get au nufe to bye a smale present for you. Yors sisiley.

I was so touched by these letters, some of which are shown on the adjacent pages, and the effort they must have put into them that I took them home every night and wrote short letters in reply. It helped with their reading as well as writing. Incidentally I had a letter from Peter when I contacted the Newham Recorder in 1986 with a photo of the class wondering where they all were. He was not actually in the photo, being absent that day. He wrote in a very good hand:

> I will try and jog your memory of who I am. I am the one who brought you tea in a Tizer bottle on opening day. I once went and got you a bag of coke for your fire, and took it to your flat in Ilford that you shared with another teacher from Carpenters Road. The flat had a hat shop at ground level and a hairdresser's above it. I have so many memories of that flat, like when Joey Olroy and I went out into a nearby street and took blossoms off a tree to give to you and when Derek Westrop and Billy Gormer and I all had a bath at the flat. It was the first real bath we had seen.

He went on to give me information about some of the class. I do remember Peter and Joe Olroy getting me a bag of coke. It was a very cold winter and fuel was in short supply. I let them leave school very promptly and they

Dear miss
all the boys sed are you going
to were your p.T cloce pleae

from Charles

answer

PT Clothes

Three Mills School
Stratford
Lodon E.15
5-2-47

Dear. Miss.
　　　　　I am Writen thes littey
to you. When wall you hav yor
Shots on at P.T.

Dear M^{ss} Hicks　From
　　　　　　　　　Fred
　　　　　Are you going to
bring your P.T. clothes on
Thursday.
　　　　Love Ruby

Three Mills School
　　Straford. E.15
　　21.2.47.
Dear Miss Hicks
　　　　　　When we have drill
Will you put you dilling clos on
and some of the girls will put on
our dilling clos love from Hilda
　　xx xx x xx x x x x

THREE MILLS SCHOOL, STRATFORD

Apologies

Dear Miss Hicks
         Just a few lines to let you no that you are a very nice teacher please miss Hicks I try to be good when you go out but it is the others they make a nos they wont be quiet I will turn over a new leafe from now on
         x x x x Yours sincerely x x x x
         From Gerald Schirn

Dear Miss Hicks,
         I am vere sorrey for bein a nusar to you but I am coing to ton twarn over a new leaf, and I hop you will answer my letter.
         Lous Derek

three Mills schools
Dear Miss
         I an verysorry that I hav been nuisances this week
         from Joe

THEE MILL
CLA4L
lan
stuffn

Dear Miss Hicks,
         I hope you are all right and hope that you will forgive me for being noisy boy
         HA HA HA HA sind
         Peter Andrew

> Dear Miss Hicks
> I hope you will get this note I am sending you. Will you trie and get some laceinpaper for me Plese
> from
> Fred
> answer

> Dear miss
> I am macking up my one somes and will you marck them
> Charles
> to
> miss

> Dear miss
> I took the trobel to by a pen and as soon as I put it down it was gon and If I dont get it back I will tell my father to come and see miss nofel a bout it and it cost me 6d.
> from charlie
> anser
> pleace

> Three Mills school
> Stratford
> 13-2-45. 15
> Dear Miss
> I hope you will get the note I am santen you will you mice & nofer Pillar box be cos they go toun it and rine the notes
> from
> Fred

> Dear Miss Hicks
> Thank you for your letter but I would like to have another spelling bee
> Yours trealy
> Jean Threxhall

queued up at the Gas, Light and Coke Company and returned with a large bag of coke. I am not sure how much it weighed but it filled a hundredweight coal sack. We then took it on a bus, stacking it under the stairs, back to our flat in Ilford Lane. That episode has been talked about many times since, particularly when the severe winter of '47 is mentioned.

The 'flat' in Ilford was actually the back part of two shops, as Peter said, with the hat shop, Fagin's, on the ground floor and a hairdresser's upstairs. I remained friends with Peggy Temple, the teacher from Carpenters Road School, and during the Easter Holidays we moved into the 'flat'. Peggy knew some of my pupils as they had previously been to Carpenters Road. I sometimes had groups of my pupils at 'Fagin's', ostensibly for extra tuition, but I think that the boys in particular just came for a good time. I remember them splashing about in the bath. They had gone to explore the property and before we knew it they had stripped off and were jumping up and down in the bath as if they were at the seaside.

In the summer, Peggy and I took both our classes to Epping Forest and Regents Park Zoo. What a risk we both took. There were about forty children for just the two of us and we travelled by public transport, on a Sunday. Peter wrote:

> Do you remember when we all met at Stratford Broadway. You took us out into the country for the day. Up to then the only greenery we had seen was the sewer bank. Thank you for that day.

Thank you Peter, for remembering.

Mention of the sewer bank brings back more strong memories. The 'Northern Outfall' ran very close to the school and was accessible by a few steps, but we didn't know of it as the Northern Outfall then. It was a narrow strip of raised ground, which ran through West Ham, roughly in a northwesterly to southeasterly direction, terminating at Barking Creek. It served more than the purpose for which it was designed, which was to enclose the channel carrying sewage to the treatment works at Barking Creek and to the outfall on the Thames. It was more than a bank enclosing sewage; it was a life-line, an artery, and whilst I was at Three Mills, it gave us as much pleasure I am sure, as the 'playing fields of Eton.'

The West Ham School Sports Association organized a scheme, which we knew as 'non competitive sports'. The object was to achieve a certain standard in four events and then to be the proud possessor of a certificate. There was a choice of two running events, also high jump, long jump, and hop step and jump. I had last performed myself, successfully, at the Russell School, in 1937 and 1938, and can remember entering when at the Bidder Street School. We had no playing fields there and were put through our paces at the Memorial Recreation ground. I remember not having any plimsolls and being handed a pair for the hundred yards event. They were too large, and one fell off whilst I was running. I am not sure whether I was awarded a certificate. If I was, I no longer have it, but I do have the ones awarded in 1937 and 1938.

The time now came for me to give my class the opportunity of being awarded a certificate, too. We practised hop step and jump, long jump, and high jump, in the hall. I put great stress on the importance of having plimsolls that fit, and the wearing of shorts. But where could we practise the hundred yards and the hundred and fifty yards? 'On the sewer bank, Miss,' I was told. Of course! Why didn't I think of it? So day after day, we went up there. I justified the frequent trips by combining the exercise with arithmetic lessons. Rather a grand explanation for an enjoyable trip out, but also a way of keeping them busy at the same time. We wrote out the 'sums' beforehand. We had to measure the length of the track. How many railings do we need? If there are twelve railings in one yard, how many in 'x' yards. How many sections of railings do we need? The sewer bank was a wide track then, like a running track, stretching from the railings on one side, to the railings on the other. I bought a stopwatch and those not running could watch the hand move round and would shout encouragement to the runners. I don't remember coming across any member of the public in those days. We had a great time, and I am pleased to say everybody received a certificate.

The only other time I had been on the sewer bank was September 7th 1940 with Rene, when we reached it via the cut, or Channelsea, a little further to the east, on our way home from Epping Forest. I could not relate the two sections when I was at Three Mills School. They could have been miles apart, in different countries even, and traversed by two different people. I recently rediscovered the sewer bank when I walked along the Channelsea Path with my husband John, and came across 'The Greenway', now a green footpath and cycleway, snaking across West Ham. The two stretches of the sewer bank, which in my mind were completely separated, having served two different purposes, now merged into one. Remarkably, the same railings are still there, although many of them are concealed by bushes. We went there on a very hot day, when the temperature was around eighty degrees. I had already walked about five miles in that heat and should have been exhausted, but I was carried along by my excitement. I touched the railings and counted them for several yards. I think that section of the sewer bank deserves a plaque, 'Along this stretch, in the spring of 1947, a class of children from the nearby Three Mills School (now demolished) practised their running skills, and in so doing, each was awarded a certificate for their achievement.'

THREE MILLS SCHOOL, STRATFORD

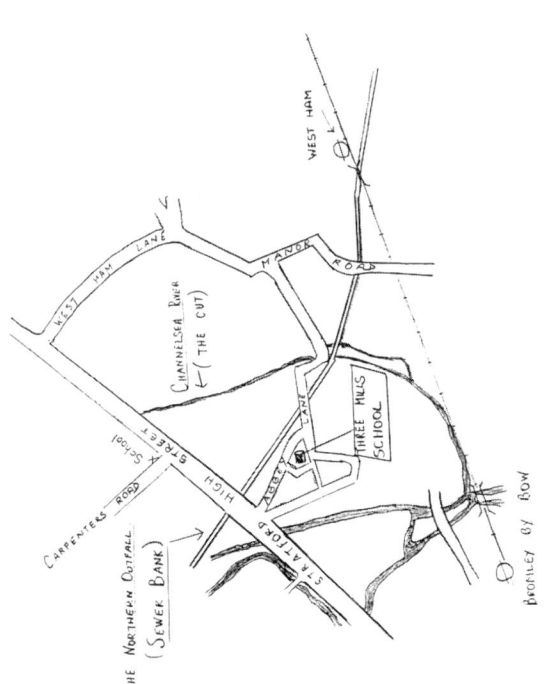

Lower Lea Project

Showing Channelsea Path, Greenway – (Sewer Bank), and Manor Road.

Location of Three Mills school and its position in relation to the Lower Lea Project.

That was a very busy year for me and I doubt whether I could have kept up the pressure for any length of time. I kept some evening classes going, but the last drama production I was in was in October 1946. That Christmas was my last at the Russell Old Students' club and the last Christmas at Bancroft. Vera went to Teacher Training College and Ferdy commenced the one-year emergency teacher-training course at Easter. Until I moved with Peggy Temple to Ilford at Easter, I kept up my Bancroft activities, but then Ferdy was not available to run the club anyway. About that time, I discovered that I could receive the F.E.T.S. grant for a year before going to university, in order to study full-time for the intermediate B.Sc. (Econ.) examination. The South East Essex Technical College ran a suitable course for their sixth form pupils, and although I was then approaching twenty three, I applied, was accepted and commenced there in September 1947.

So a further chapter in our lives was coming to an end, as I was embarking on another. I doubt if Bancroft was ever the same again. Ferdy wrote to me in 1996:

> Wise counsellors tell us not to go back. Last Saturday I went to Canning Town Library and from there took a winding trail through the new Canning Town and Custom House. I noted a general improvement, but the area was unrecognisable and I could only navigate by using street names. This took me to Bancrofts. The outside had been pebble-dashed years ago and looked it and the oak panelled doors replaced by heavy roller-shutters. A shabby notice declared that it was, or had been, ' Bancrofts Social Club (Free House).' All surrounding buildings were gone, so I was able to get round the back to prise open the lop-sided door. The scene inside was awful. All fittings, panelling, wall-bars etc. were gone and more recent wall coverings were torn and peeling. The place was full of rubbish. The ceilings were about to capitulate to gravity. I caught a bus back to the Greengate and walked to the Boleyn, but by this time, I'd had enough.

So, the building was derelict and soon to be demolished. What about the boys? I hope they remember those days with as much pleasure as I do. It did help to open up another world for them, as it did for me.

Three Mills Senior School closed in 1965, but the building remained until the nineties, when, like Bancroft's, it too was demolished. A strange coincidence occurred before that. In the eighties, my son John decided to read for a degree in Sociology, and went to the North East London Polytechnic. This was formerly the Stratford Municipal College where I had spent many evenings, some of them in the air-raid shelter, studying for the

Matriculation examination. The newly named 'N.E.L.P.' was short of space, so some lectures were held at the local school.. It had to be, of course, Three Mills School. As we were living in Hampshire and no longer had any connection with West Ham, and John had in fact never been there, that was some coincidence. A different mother might have wished he had gone to Oxford or Cambridge, but actually I took pleasure in the fact that he had selected N.E.L.P.

In their notes in the class letterbox, some of the children asked if their work was improving. It certainly was and I am sure it continued to improve beyond measure after I had left. Charlie sent me a photo of himself taken in 1985, receiving a 'photographer of the year award.' Peter had a spell in the Rifle Brigade as a P.T. Instructor. In 1986 he was managing a football team and was interested in history. Hilda's son was a teacher. I didn't doubt their potential when I taught them, only wondered whether they would have the opportunity to reach it. In their later letters to me many of them expressed a wish for a reunion, but unfortunately I found this too difficult to organize from a distance. That was a pity.

Our 'running track' no longer looks down on to the school, but on to houses that my class and I could not have imagined then. I still have an affection for Three Mills and am delighted at the Heritage Scheme in the

Top row: Leonard Askew, Mary St Piere, Derek Westrop, Derek Thick, Joe Olroy.
Middle row: Billy Gomer, Roy Bissett, Dennis Marriott, Charles Bowes, Marie Hill, Gladys Squires, Phyllis Kemp, Marie Smith, June Nash.
Bottom row: Tony Sheppard, David King, Fred Rundell, Gerald Schirn, Mary Quinlin, Jean Threakle.

area, and the Lower Lea Project. It gives me another reason for visiting the area.

I returned to Three Mills School after the summer holiday of 1947, for just two weeks, and before the beginning of term at the South East Essex Technical College, but by then, my class had moved on.

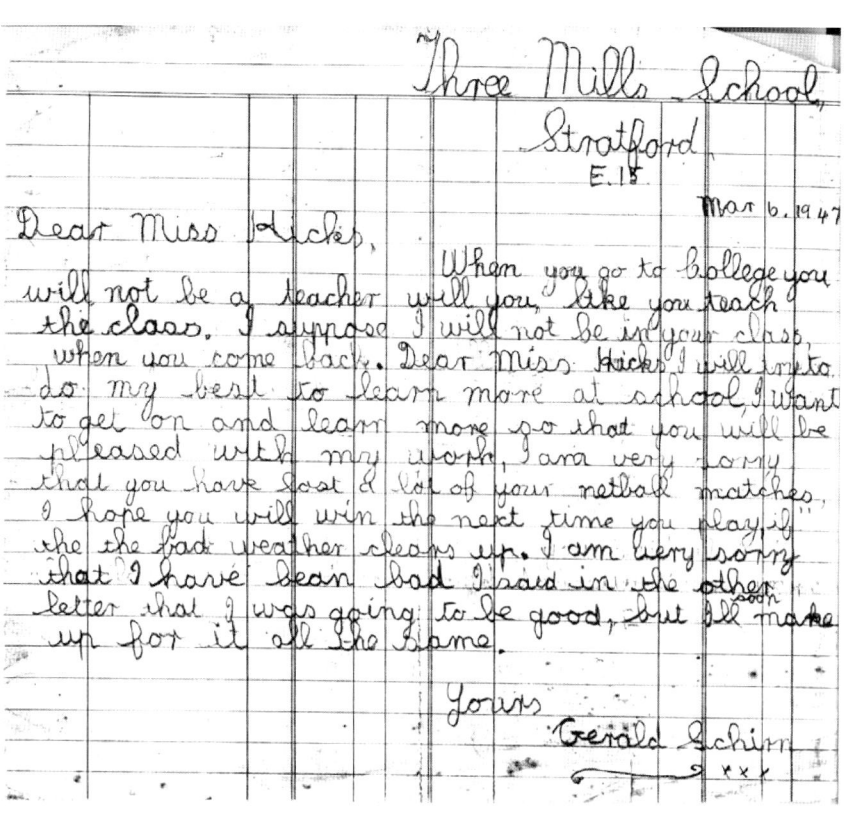

– 9 –

Fagin's Kitchen – a Happy Interlude

When I first commenced teaching in West Ham, in September 1946, I was still living at Selsdon Road. The house was rather crowded now, so gone were the days when friends could stop over, sleeping on the floor or on chairs or sometimes, even, in a bed. Pat and Eddie were there and also Marie, who was no longer in the WAAF. Jimmy, after a short period in the army, had been discharged as his hip had 'flared up' again. Also, there was now a new man in my mother's life and he, too, had moved in. Harry worked in the office at the LNER at Stratford, where my mother was employed as a cook in the staff canteen, preparing meals for railway personnel who were on shift work.

All was not sweetness and light at Selsdon Road. There were frequent arguments. Harry was harmless enough, but he did take to the bottle occasionally. My mother was ambivalent in her attitude towards him, being at times forgiving and at other times intolerant. She was not now an easy person to live with, and although she had been an exceptional and caring mother whilst we were growing up, she did not seem able to cope with us as adolescents. Lawrie had left home and Jimmy did so frequently. Perhaps it was because her own adolescence had been such a disappointment? Far from encouraging me in my endeavours she seemed to resent them, and was even, perhaps, jealous. 'You're at it again,' she would say when I was reading or trying to do homework. 'Why don't you go out and enjoy yourself like any other normal girl? When you've got your qualifications you'll forget about us.' When I was using a corner of the table for preparation or homework, she said, 'There you go. Trying to push us out again.' She seemed afraid of losing us, as if maturing, and having views of our own, would lead automatically to disaffection. She had not developed a mature relationship with her own mother so was not to know that such a relationship was possible.

This ill feeling led Marie and me to consider leaving home, but instead we had rather a bizarre arrangement. We rented a room upstairs and kept ourselves. There was also a very small room off, with a sink and a single cold tap. There was no kitchen or cooker, but a gas point, so we had a gas ring installed which was our sole heating source both for our culinary requirements and for keeping warm. There was actually a fireplace in the room, but like most grates designed for bedrooms, it was pretty useless. When I left my superannuated local government employment, I was able to cash in my contributions, and not being advised otherwise, was foolish enough to do so. I was not then aware that as a teacher, I could have continued to remain in the NALGO pension scheme, when my existing contributions and years of service would have been to my advantage. I received about forty pounds and spent it on improving the fireplace and installing a tiled surround. So we had a comfortable room, but I had sacrificed five and a half years of pension contributions in the process!

I would sometimes invite friends in for a cup of tea after we had been out and we would just sit and talk. One night, as we were all sitting round the fire, just chatting, my mother burst in, in her night attire. It was true it was about 11.30 p.m. 'What ——ing time do you call this?' she said. 'Haven't you got homes to go to? It's not a ——ing doss house.' Ferdy, Vera and Stan Roope left immediately, to my great embarrassment. I was 22 at the time.

I had remained friends with Peggy Temple from Carpenters Road School, who was then in lodgings. She had heard of accommodation becoming available, through her hairdresser, a Mr. Laut, who owned premises in Ilford Lane, Ilford. The salon was upstairs, and Fagin's hat shop was downstairs. The unfurnished accommodation consisted of two bedrooms behind the hairdresser's and a kitchen and living room behind the hat shop. He offered this to Peggy at a reasonable rent, and she was delighted, as property was very difficult to obtain then. She asked if I was interested in sharing, which indeed I was. Marie had decided to emigrate to New Zealand. She saw no reason to remain in West Ham and wanted a fresh start. My mother's sister had emigrated to New Zealand when mother was pregnant with Marie in 1923. Marie was accepted under a scheme to train as a mental nurse, under which her passage out would be paid for. She had to agree to remain for two years. She was then waiting for the date of her departure.

So, in March 1947, the three of us moved into Ilford Lane. I was sorry to leave Pat and Eddie, but looked forward to having my own home. Peggy and I bought some second-hand furniture, curtains and carpets and soon made ourselves comfortable. One Saturday, my grandmother arrived, unannounced, in a van, with some more second-hand furniture, which she had purchased for us. She was seventy-eight years old and had come a long way from Westbourne Park.

Marie was twenty-four in April and planned to sail to New Zealand in May. Before she left we held a birthday party cum leaving party for her. Those present included Gran and our former next-door neighbour George Fowler and his young daughter. There was also Ferd and Vera and the Kerr brothers, Jim, George and Bill, all three members of the SPGB. Bob Macnish, a Russell 'Old Student' and Bancroft friend, also came to bid

Marie farewell. Together with brother Jimmy, who was living with us, and a girl friend from her WAAF days, this represented a cross-section of friends and family of both Marie and myself. Sadly there was no mother or father, Lawrie, Patricia or Eddie. Shortly afterwards, Peggy and I waved Marie off from Liverpool Street station, where she caught the boat train which was to take her to Tilbury and then half way round the world. It was to be forty years before we met again. As we drank a cup of tea on her arrival at Heathrow airport, we looked across the table at each other. There we were, two elderly ladies in our sixties, wondering where all the years had gone.

After Marie left, Peggy and I continued to create a pleasant home for ourselves. We hit it off from the start. We worked very well together and never once had cross words. It was such a relief. We were very seldom on our own, though. Soon after Marie left, Stan Roope asked if he could move into the small second bedroom which Marie had used. He was about six years older than us and had joined the SPGB the same evening as Ferdy, Vera and me. He was a Russell Old Student and Bancroft helper, and we had mutual friends, so there was no problem. We ate together most of the time and shared expenses amicably. He stayed for several months.

Friends were always welcome to drop in at 83, Ilford Lane, our new address. It was quite close to Ilford Station, opposite which, on the corner of Station Road and Ilford Hill, the SPGB held public meetings on a Friday night. There was quite a wide pavement at that point and it was an excellent place for public meetings. The outdoor platform in those days was used chiefly for the expression of minority viewpoints and the level of discussion was generally high. Anybody trying to be frivolous was usually dealt with swiftly but good-naturedly. We were often mistaken for the Communist Party. Just after the war there was some disquiet about the fact that Russian women who had married British men, civil servants, embassy staff and the like, were not allowed to leave Russia. A favourite question was, 'What about the Russian brides?' This question surfaced for many years, for which, of course, we had no answer or responsibility.

There were more people on the streets of an evening then, prepared to engage in debate or just listen to a lively exchange of views. There was no television to tempt people to stay in to watch the latest serial or 'soap'. Gone were the days when speakers just stood on a soapbox or orange crate. They now stood on properly constructed, fairly high platforms, which folded easily for storage. And where better to store the Station Road platform than 'round the back' behind Fagin's. Every Friday night the platform would be collected. There was usually an introductory speaker whose job it was to gather a crowd, and then to hand over to the appointed speaker. They would keep going for several hours, and if the meeting was a success, there would be groups of people in discussion afterwards. The SPGB had many excellent speakers, some of them going back for a good number of years and they had had plenty of time to perfect their technique. After the meetings at Station Road, the platform would be returned, accompanied by several people, still bent on discussion, particularly if a cup of tea was available as well. Peggy and I would get to bed very late on Friday nights. No members had cars then, so it was important they knew the times of the trains or buses, or could manage to walk home. The name of the hat shop below seemed most appropriate, and our abode soon became known as 'Fagin's Kitchen'.

Another good place for meetings, locally, was on the corner outside the 'Cock Hotel', High Street North, East Ham. Sadly this has now been demolished to make way for a bank and offices and no public meetings are held there now. In fact, outdoor platform discussions are a thing of the past. They were a good vehicle for the exchange of ideas. We have mass demonstrations now and party political broadcasts on television, rather than lively but reasoned argument on street corners and in parks.

That year, my first year of teaching, was certainly a hectic one for me, and when the end of the school year arrived at the end of July, I was ready for a break. Peggy and I went to Martham for two weeks and stayed with her parents. All their water was obtained from a well, but Peggy's mother ran the house as efficiently as if she'd had all modern conveniences. We slept late every morning and had a 'full English breakfast' in bed every day. Norfolk was a new and pleasant experience for me. We spent many hours sun-bathing on the beach at Hemsby. One day we went to visit Peggy's two elderly maiden aunts, or rather, great-aunts, who lived in a rambling old house with a stone floor and no running water, in another village. These two elderly great-aunts must have been in their late seventies and were the last remaining members of a family of five. Peggy's mother, was their only niece, and her brother Bert was the only nephew. These five were the illegitimate offspring of the fourth Earl of Orford, a descendant of the Prime Minister, Sir Robert Walpole. In his later years he had had a liaison with his young servant girl. He looked after her well and made some provision for her when he died, which included the cottage which Peggy and I visited. It was no secret in the village apparently and the old great-aunts' mother proudly rode about in a horse and carriage. Peggy's mother was a very prudish woman and when the last of the old aunts died she was so ashamed of the illegitimate connection that she destroyed all the old photos, much to Peggy's distress. The cottage passed to Bert's widow Ivy, and when she died Peggy had a half share, so it had to be sold. There's a fascinating story there to be told. Peggy did some research, but never got round to writing it all up.

When we returned to Fagin's at the end of the holiday, we found brother Jimmy had moved in, having left home again. He had been very unsettled since being discharged from the army for medical reasons, and had not been able to find a suitable job. He was now fit again, or so he thought, but before long, he was back again in hospital.

Before returning to Three Mills School for two weeks at the beginning of September '47 and prior to going to the South East Essex Technical College, I made a trip to Ireland with sister Pat, who was then fourteen years old. It was the long school summer break and Pat was keen on the idea. At first, Peggy and I planned to go, crossing from Holyhead to Dublin on Monday, 25th August, but were unable to get sailing tickets, so abandoned the idea. At the last moment return tickets became available from Liverpool to Dublin from Thursday, 28th August until the following Tuesday. By then, however, Peggy had alternative plans. I was still keen to go and Pat was happy to join me, although we were rather daunted at the thought of hitchhiking.. We had to travel that way for financial reasons. My mother was hesitant to agree to the idea at first, but was eventually persuaded. In spite of our difference of opinion at times, she did accept that I was capable of taking care of Pat. We had very little money, of course, which was nothing new, and we would be staying in Youth Hostels. The Youth Hostel movement was a brilliant creation and made it possible for people in our circumstances to travel. We could not have done it any other way. For a few shillings a night, and self-catering, the countryside was opened up to us, provided we could walk or occasionally hitch a lift. It never occurred to me that there was any danger involved. I found that long-distance lorry drivers were often bored and enjoyed company on the journey, and I thought it incumbent on me to keep up a conversation with them, which we both enjoyed. It might have been risky for a lone woman hitchhiker, but I never tried that.

Pat and I started out on Monday 25th August and planned to make our way to Manchester, where a friend from the SPGB was to put us up for the night before crossing to Dublin on the Thursday. I kept an account of the lifts we had, and they make interesting reading. We started hitching from St. Albans, where a lorry driver took us to Birmingham, from where a schoolmistress drove us direct to the hostel at Clent. The next day, Tuesday, it was bus to Kidderminster, van to Bridgenorth, lorry to Dawley, car to Newcastle-under-Lyme and then a very long walk, some of it in the dark, to the Rudyard Lake Youth Hostel. On Wednesday we had a car for one mile to a transport café at Rushton, where a lorry driver took us to Manchester, and after a long walk, we arrived at my friend Margaret's house.

All the drivers were interesting, particularly the last one. He was from a family of seven boys who before the war were all miners and they vowed never to go underground again. Of the seven, four were discharged from the army as medically unfit and could no longer work. The fifth had returned from Palestine the previous day with fractured ribs and three fingers missing, caused when a bomb was thrown into the barracks by a Jewish protester. The sixth had returned to the mines and the seventh had become a lorry driver. The previous day we'd had a driver who was both anti-Jewish and anti-German, and a commercial traveller who thought workers were lazy and had been spoilt by their period in the army. They were all pleasant people and helpful to us!

We left Audenshaw, Manchester, on Thursday, for Liverpool, supplied with sandwiches made by Margaret's mother. At the docks, we saw some soldiers disembarking, after having been to India. The third class night crossing was appalling. The boat was very crowded and noisy. People were shouting and children were crying. It took twelve hours and we arrived in Dublin at eight o'clock in the morning, after a very restless night.

We booked in at the hostel in Dublin, and on our way there we were surprised to find that we were being screamed at for wearing shorts. A crowd of children gathered menacingly behind us and several women spat, not directly at us I am pleased to say, but as a sign of disapproval. The warden of the hostel advised us not to walk around Dublin in shorts. During the few days we were in Dublin we were surprised to find items in the shops which were not available back home, such as fully-fashioned silk stockings and clothing without coupons. There was plenty of meat available, too, so we bought a huge steak, and cooked it at the hostel. There were queues however for buses and we were always pushed to the back, as priests and nuns always had priority.

On the weekend, we hitched to Glendalough, where we stayed at a delightful youth hostel and spent a pleasant few days there. Our crossing back on Tuesday night was just as unpleasant as the crossing out. Again, it took twelve hours. Cattle might have travelled in better conditions. I sympathised with the many Irish people who were working in England and made the crossing frequently to visit friends and family. On arrival at Liverpool, we had just four shillings and two pence left, partly due to my profligacy in buying four pairs of fully-fashioned pure silk stockings, at seven shillings and eleven pence a pair, so we made straight for home. We had two good lifts, and then the third and last lift was not to our liking. We were fairly near home, so when the driver stopped for a beer, we got out, not knowing where we were. We soon found out, and then took a bus to Arnos Grove, then a tube to Mile End, and a bus back home. We had no money left at all, but Pat was safely delivered. I returned to the comfort and safety of Fagin's kitchen and ate a hearty meal with Peggy and Jimmy.

FAGIN'S KITCHEN – A HAPPY INTERLUDE

We had a lift on this, a mile and a half, on our way to Glendalough.

After two more weeks at Three Mills School at the beginning of September, I commenced at the South East Essex Technical College, as a student. I received small gifts from my former pupils and the staff bought me a very good Parker fountain pen. A member of staff took a photo of us in the playground of Three Mills, which I still possess. Most teachers remember their first class and I am no exception. I have had a variety of teaching experiences since, some good, some not so good, but it is the first class of whom I retain the clearest memory.

I made quite an impression apparently when I entered the small upper sixth form of the SEETC. It consisted of about half a dozen seventeen to eighteen year old boys and until then sixth forms were made up of pupils who had been through the school, that is from the first year of secondary education. The admission of 'mature' students was an innovation introduced due to the exceptional post-war situation as regards education. I was then a lively twenty-three year old, with definite views. I had already had an introduction to the subject of economics through the SPGB, but this was 'Marxist' economics. I now found it difficult to reconcile the theory of perfect competition with the labour theory of value. I became impatient with the mathematical juggling of demand and supply curves and made remarks such as, 'What about coffee being burnt to keep up prices and fruit being dumped, when there are people short of food?' These were doubtless subjects worthy of discussion, but not in the context of the

South East Essex Technical College, July 1948

lesson in progress. I must have been a pain to the lecturers. I became friendly with one student, Seymour Broadbridge, and he, too, became a visitor to Fagin's. We both went on to the same university and remained staunch friends for the rest of his life.

When Jimmy went back to hospital at Claybury in Essex, Peggy and I would visit him at weekends, sometimes. Relations with my mother were still a little strained and on one of our visits, we came face to face. She had never met Peggy and must have had a jaundiced view of what she was like. However, Peggy was cordial and civilized and when the visit was over she invited her back to tea. We had to travel on the same bus, anyway. Back at Fagin's, Peggy found an attractive table cloth, and set the table with a pot of tea, a plate of sandwiches and a plate of cakes in the centre. My mother was quite impressed. 'This is very nice,' she said, with a slight catch in her voice. 'Thank you.' My mother was like the little girl, who had a curl right in the middle of her forehead, and when she was good...

That broke the ice, I was pleased to say and then came Christmas. Jimmy was allowed home from hospital for a few days. The three of us were invited to the home of the three brothers Kerr for Christmas day. They had a wonderful mother who was nearly bent double with arthritis. Relations with Selsdon Road must have been harmonious, because on Boxing Day, Peggy and I were the hostesses. We cooked a roast chicken dinner for fifteen people, including Mum, Harry, Pat, Eddie, Jimmy, Vera and Ferdy, George and Bill Kerr, Jim Kerr and his future wife Marjorie, who was then at college with Vera, Barry McCallum and Bob Macnish, two friends from the Russell and Bancroft days. I can't think where we all sat.

Bob Macnish was a very warm, kind and considerate person. He had been a Warrant Officer in the Air Force and was keen to be more than just a friend, but I was too impatient and single-minded to reciprocate. He kept up his interest for several years. I must have unintentionally hurt him emotionally, part of the pain of growing up, I suppose, which we all experience. He gave me a copy of 'The Rubaiyat of Omar Khayyam', hoping, I think, that I would heed its message, but it was not one that I was then willing to accept. Life was beset with too many problems and injustices, for me to contemplate reclining,

> Here with a loaf of bread beneath the bough,
> A flask of wine, a book of verse – and thou
> Beside me singing in the Wilderness –
> And the wilderness is paradise enow.

I was not happy with the sentiment of 'live for today and don't worry about the future.'

> Ah, fill the cup: – what boots it to repeat.
> How time is slipping underneath our feet:
> Unborn tomorrow, and dead yesterday,
> Why fret about them if today be sweet!

But now, with the benefit of hindsight, I can appreciate why the *Rubaiyat* may have been popular with servicemen, who must sometimes have wondered if there would be a tomorrow. My husband, John, remembers with nostalgia one of his army colleagues, Corporal Joe Sims, knowing and reciting it all through. He preferred it to those long recitations from others of, 'He had an arm just like a leg, my brother Sylvest'. At that time, however, I was thinking about my future, and hoped to play some part in shaping it, so I could not agree, either, with:

> The moving finger writes; and having writ,
> Moves on; nor all thy piety nor wit
> Shall lure it back to cancel half a line,
> or all thy tears wash out a word of it.

I must admit, however, that whilst not agreeing with its philosophy, I have gained more pleasure from reading the book since, than I did then, when I was struggling to come to an understanding of Marxism.

That year, Peggy and I had been going to economics classes run by Ted Wilmot of the SPGB. He was dealing with the first nine chapters of Marx's *Capital*. I found it very difficult and did not learn much beyond the first few chapters. One evening, in the spring of '48, in a café where we all met afterwards, he passed us a note. 'I've nowhere to live. Do you know where I could put up for the night?' He was in his forties and had two adult children, both in the SPGB. His marriage latterly had been stormy and he was no longer living at home. Well, we were sitting ducks. We said he could come home with us for the night. There wasn't much room, as Jimmy was there, too. He slept in the living room. We didn't know it then, but that was the beginning of a lasting and happy relationship with Peggy.

Ted had a remarkable mind and had been in the SPGB since his twenties and although he did speak and debate at public meetings on occasions, he devoted himself principally to the exposition of economics and philosophy. When he was not at work, as an electrician for the GPO, he would be reading or writing or preparing a lecture, all the time rolling his own cigarettes, so absentmindedly that there was more tobacco down the front of his shirt than in the cigarette. He had a pot of tea stewing continuously and we learnt not to say 'Yes, please' when he offered us a cup.

That Easter I was invited to stay with a pen friend from Mons, with whom I had been corresponding to improve my French. That was my first trip abroad, and I travelled very lightly, with just a small holdall. We were not allowed any foreign currency, then, so I went over with nothing. I was very well received as the people of Mons had fond memories of the 'Tommies', and considered me as their representative. I was given a tour of the British cemetery at Mons and what a depressing sight that was. That was my first experience of a cemetery to the war dead. There were rows upon uniform rows of headstones. My pen friend's parents invited people round, and they wanted me to sing First World War songs. They had a piano, and I played, very badly, 'Pack up your troubles', and 'It's a long way to Tipperary', etc. We all sang, and they loved it.

After Easter I started to prepare for the Intermediate B Sc. (Econ.) examination and then we had some bad news in June. Mr. Laut our landlord gave us notice to leave. Fagin's, the milliners, were leaving. Mr. Laut had put up their rent, which they could not afford, so they had to leave. He wanted to let the shop with accommodation. This was a very worrying time for all of us, especially me, as I had to sit the exam the first week in July. The future was very uncertain. I wasn't sure I would pass the exam, and if I did, whether I would get a university place, and if I did, whether or not I would have to be resident.

By the end of term, we had not been able to resolve the situation, so in desperation, we just packed up. The mother of one of Peggy's pupils took some furniture and I rented the downstairs middle room from my mother, so there was room there for my single bed and a chair. Ted found lodgings somewhere and Jimmy went to brother Lawrie's. Peggy arranged lodgings in Ravenhill Road, off Selsdon Road and then Peggy and I set out on a hiking tour of France, to put our cares behind us. We had £42 between us, plus a return ticket each to Dieppe. So that was the end of Fagin's kitchen.

We were very sad at having to leave Fagin's. We had been very happy there. It had been the first home of our own for each of us and we never ever forgot it. We were so close that Party members referred to us as 'Peg-and-Ivy', not always knowing which was which. Fifty years later I met a fellow member on the sea front at Brighton, when the Labour Party conference was on. He said, 'Hello. Peggy-or-Ivy, isn't it?' Some people outside our immediate group of friends, wondered if we were lesbians. I had never even heard of the word then. No. We were just very good friends, and remained so for the rest of Peggy's life.

– 10 –

A Trip to Post-war France

When we set out for France on the 9th August 1948, we had no firm plans. We just wanted to see as much of post-war France as we could, with what little money we had. Our entire luggage was carried in a rucksack, which in those days was not very well designed and was not much more than a holdall with shoulder straps. I bought a pair of stout boots from a second-hand shop, and, at first, that was my only footwear. We had a minimum of clothing, which we kept washed at the Youth Hostels. We had a map of the Youth Hostels in France, and it was their location which really determined our plan. I was uncertain what my future would be at the end of the holiday, as I had not yet received my exam result. It would be sent to Selsdon Road, so I asked my mother to forward my post to the Youth Hostel in Paris where we hoped to stay.

We left Victoria for Dieppe at 8.30. a.m. That was Peggy's first trip abroad but I had been to Mons the previous Easter. Dieppe was a very bustling port and we were soon approached by a Frenchman who offered to take us by car to the Youth Hostel. His intentions were probably perfectly honourable, but we were very much on our guard at that stage, so declined. We walked to the hostel where we met four young men from England, just setting out on a cycle trip of France. We shared a meal with them of bread and cheese, washed down with wine, which the French hostellers were always ready to offer us. That evening was a very lively one at the hostel, with singing and dancing and the occasional glass of wine. We were to discover that most evenings at the hostels were like this. As in the UK, there was a curfew at 10.30, when the warden, or 'mère-aub' as she was known in France, turned the lights out. We carried on by the light of torches and bicycle lamps, until 2 a.m, when the 'mère-aub' descended on us in a torrent of highly-charged French, which apparently meant that we were most unreasonable, we should be ashamed of ourselves and would we go to bed immediately. She was right, of course, but we had enjoyed our first night in France.

The next day Peggy and I got a lift in a lorry to Rouen, where there was still evidence of the destruction of the war years. The cathedral, in particular, and the area surrounding it, still bore the scars of that conflict, as did many of the cities we visited. The four English cyclists were also at Rouen

War damaged Rouen cathedral

and in fact we stayed together for the next week and made an arrangement that whoever arrived at the hostel first would organize a meal. After a quick snack, we decided to eat together that evening, and then went out for some provisions. I thought soup and bread would be good for starters and, remembering my mother's skill at the stewpot, called in at a butcher's for some bones, out of which I first planned to make some stock. There was a huge saucepan at the hostel, the kind used in restaurants and I put the bones on to simmer gently whilst we shopped for the rest of the ingredients. When I returned, there was much interest in the simmering bones and when I explained their purpose, there was a great deal of scepticism and disbelief. When the soup was ready, it wasn't just Peggy, me, and the four lads who were interested in it. There was also a young Frenchman there, whose acquaintance I had made at the hostel in Dieppe. Just as we were about to enjoy the soup somebody remarked that the stock had been made from horse bones. Nobody minded, except one of the cyclists, but the Frenchman, a young schoolteacher from Strasbourg, asked for more. That evening, we danced and chatted until lights out. There must have been something in those there bones.

The next day we made for Vernon and were fairly soon given a lift by a very poor family in a ramshackle car. They were going to Evreux, which was off our main route and offered to take us home with them, but we preferred to stay at the hostel. They were a wonderful family and when we left we gave them two tins of Nescafé which we had brought with us, as we understood it was in short supply in France. We were still some distance from Vernon, and we set out, walking. We didn't actually 'thumb' for lifts, but as we set out on foot, drivers would stop and ask if we wanted a lift. French people then, just after the war, were still pro-English and everybody we met couldn't do enough for us. Our walk took us past an airfield, where we chatted, of course, with some airmen, who gave us a bottle of wine. Later, being thirsty, I drank rather too much and became light-headed. I had a lot to learn. We soon picked up a lift in an Army lorry, which took us to Pacy, where a parson, who spoke English with an Oxford accent, took us right to the door of the hostel. It had once been a school. The warden there was a young Rumanian student, and as there was nobody else at the hostel he took Peggy shopping for supplies for a meal whilst I manned the hostel and awaited the arrival of our four cyclist friends

After the seven of us had a good meal, the four lads and Peggy and I went out for the evening and found a delightful hotel, Hotel Normandie. It was empty except for us and there were six revolving stools at the counter and we each took one. We didn't know what to drink but we thought we ought to do what the French did. We started out with beer and then discovered that Calvados was on offer, 'made from apples', so that seemed harmless enough. After three or four, I didn't know whether I was revolving or whether it was the stool and the others were in a similar state. We just managed to slide down from the stools and make our way out, where we staggered back to the hostel. Some more hostellers had arrived by then and the warden had invited some locals in for singing and dancing. They invited us to join in. We tried to, but were incapable, so we found a patch of grass outside, and flopped out. I was a bit further up the learning curve by now, but not quite there. I did learn the French word 'saoul'.

Eating grapes in Vernon with the four cyclists.

'Bathroom' at Suresnes

We were foolish enough to visit the Hotel Normandie the following day. This time I was sick, and what a horrible feeling it was. I had reached the top of the learning curve. I have not touched calvados since.

The following day we took a train to Paris. I was anxious to find out whether any post had arrived for me and we hoped to stay at the Youth Hostel. Unfortunately it was full, and furthermore there was no post for me. We were directed to a hostel at Suresnes, in a rural area to the west of Paris, quite close to the Bois de Boulogne. This turned out to be a delightful place to stay. It was set in a wood and consisted of five tents for males and a small stone building for females, which Peggy and I had to ourselves. There were no toilet facilities, just a trench behind some sacking amongst the trees, so we always went there together, with one to 'keep cave.' We washed by a standpipe, which fed into a concrete trough, and cooked in the open, by lighting bits of wood under some wire mesh.

The next day we had arranged to meet Ferdy, Vera and Barry at the Paris hostel where they had intended to stay after being in Switzerland for two weeks. So again we went into Paris. Still no post for me and no room at the inn for our friends, so they joined us at Suresnes for a few days. By then, Peggy and I had 'bonded' with the four lads. One evening we all went to the Folies Bergères. I didn't know what sort of show it was. It seemed to be very popular, as there were crowds fighting to get in. There were no orderly queues, and people were pushing and jostling, including us. Eventually we reached the front of the crowd and were let in. We had seats very high up in the balcony, but even from that distance, I could see it was quite a daring performance for those times.

Shortly after that, Peggy was taken ill with pains in her chest. She could hardly move. Maguey, the young woman who looked after the hostel, took care of her. She improved slightly and was able to travel with us to Paris the next day, where we planned to go up the Eiffel Tower. We didn't hitch on these occasions. There was a very good, reasonably cheap train service from Suresnes. Unfortunately, in Paris, after a 'citron pressé', she was taken ill again. One of our friends, Johnny Churchill, who was very fond of Peggy, returned with her to Suresnes. Two lads went off to the Trocadero and promised to meet Reg White and me at the Tower. They didn't turn up, so in the end, only two of us made it to the top. Reg and I were very hungry, and on the way up we passed some ham rolls for sale. It was freezing cold when we reached the top. We took a quick photo and then Reg turned to me and said, 'Oh, Ivy. I've had enough of the Eiffel Tower. Shall we go down and get one of those ham rolls we passed on the way up?' We couldn't get down quickly enough, but the ham rolls had gone. That's all I remember about the Eiffel Tower.

Peggy had improved sufficiently by the evening to come with us and a group of hostellers and locals from the village, to the local bistro, 'Au Papillon'. There were so many people trying to get in that, once we were in, the doors were closed. We had a wonderful time. There were a variety of nationalities present, French and English of course, but also Belgian and Dutch. We sat round very large tables and I think there were only two choices of wine, red or white, and it cost practically nothing. The procedure was to buy a few bottles, or carafes, and to place them on the table and make them available to everybody. Sometimes the proprietor would place wine on the table at no cost if he thought the supply was getting low. We sang patriotic and sentimental songs, danced a little, and conversed as best we could and I came to realize that the locals had started to celebrate the anniversary of 'La Libération' which had taken place just three years previously. It was still fresh in their minds. Some of the French were very emotionally charged because of their experiences during the occupation. We were very popular, that evening, being English. We stayed until 2 a.m. and then all walked back through the village to the hostel, singing all the way.

The next day the four lads had to return home and we were sorry to see them go. We'd formed quite a pleasant relationship in the short time we had known each other. Reg White and Johnny Churchill were keen to continue the friendship and did indeed correspond with Peggy and me for quite a while, but events prevented us from ever meeting up again. After we saw them off, we then travelled with Ferd, Vera and Barry for a few days. We stayed first in a hostel at Tours, which was in a magnificent château and then went on to Blois. They returned to Suresnes with us before departing for home.

Peggy and I stayed at Suresnes for a few more days. There was plenty of company and talk at the hostel, and there was always somebody cooking or brewing up and food and drink was always being handed around. Several men fell madly in love with Peggy and me. There was Marcel who first saw Peggy at 'Au Papillon' and was delighted to meet her again. He saw us in the early hours of the morning as Ferd, Vera and Barry were preparing to depart. We were struggling to get a fire going to help prepare breakfast for them, as they had a train to catch, but it was pouring with rain. Marcel and his two Belgian friends had just arrived and they soon managed to light the fire and brew up, but it was too late for our West Ham friends.

Marcel, Jean and Gerard, the two Belgians, had been in Paris all night, dancing and celebrating 'La Liberation' of three years previously, as well they might. Marcel had been in the French resistance and had taken part in the successful uprising in Paris on the 19th August 1944. He later took us for a short walk to a spot at the back of the hostel and showed us some stone monumental crosses marking the spots where French 'maquis' were put to death by the Germans. He also showed us a torture chamber where the maquis were tortured until they gave information.

He was very sentimental and mourned the loss of many of his friends. He had never really settled down after the war. I think he went from hostel to hostel living 'off his wits'. He fell madly in love with Peggy and shed a tear when we left. So did the two young Belgians who became infatuated with me. When they left Gerard gave me a photo of himself and Jean took a red spotted scarf from his neck, and gave it to me and said, 'Keep this forever.' There must have been something in the water at Suresnes, as a Tunisian medical student was also besotted with me. He assumed I was an American as he thought all English girls were 'reserved'. He said he first noticed me when I was struggling to get the fire going in the rain. He followed me about everywhere, even to the local market, where I had gone to buy a pair of sandals. Actually, he was very useful there as he spoke French fluently and was able to haggle with the salesman. He brought the price down from 750 francs to 700 francs. The rate of exchange then was 864 francs to the pound sterling. After we left, he obtained my address from the French Youth Hostels Association and wrote to me.

Another admirer was Peter Senn, an Anglo-Indian Oxford undergraduate. Actually, Peggy and I spent a day with Marcel and Peter at Versailles. Whilst there, and not having eaten very well for a few days, we were obliged to eat, what we thought then, was an expensive meal. It turned out to be one of the best meals I had had at that time. We had as much soup as we could eat, steak, chips and salad, buttered rolls, peach melba and cream, and champagne, brought to the table in a bucket of ice and all served up by a very attentive waiter. I had never had such a meal before. It cost 1000 francs each, not much more than the sandals had cost me.

By now we were getting short of cash and we thought we should return home but Marcel had other ideas. Having been in the French resistance he knew how to survive on practically nothing. The four of us hitched to Lille where we stayed at the Youth Hostel. We were well received, as Marcel knew the warden. From there, Peter left for home, but we went across

At the Belgium–France crossing, with coffee in my rucksack

the border into Belgium with Marcel. The idea was to buy as much coffee as our rucksacks would hold. We then had a long walk to return to the border at a point where Marcel knew a friendly Customs Officer. We successfully performed this operation and then sold the coffee to an Algerian restaurant owner that he knew, at a considerably higher price. Strangely, coffee was in short supply and expensive in France, but readily obtainable and cheaper in Belgium. We repeated the performance just one more time but crossed the border at a different point. I like to think we did nobody any harm. The coffee seller in Belgium was glad of the business, Josef, the Algerian, was able to serve coffee in his restaurant and we stayed in France for another week. My conscience was at ease.

Josef prepared a substantial meal for us and that was the first time I had tasted couscous. I was also offered a coffee, but at that time I had never drunk coffee, as I did not like it. The only coffee I knew was 'Camp' coffee essence in a bottle. When I refused, he said, 'Try it with a cognac. You might like it that way.' I'd never had cognac either and didn't know what it was. However, I tried it with freshly made coffee, and yes, I liked it. Another addition to my cuisine was globe artichokes. Marcel gathered several of these from a field and cooked them at the hostel. We peeled off the leaves, one by one, and dipped the fleshy base in oil, vinegar and garlic and then sucked this off the fibrous leaf. It seemed a long-winded business for such a small amount of food, but it was very tasty. It was more than a food. It was a social occasion, too. The preparation, the cooking, the communal supply of artichokes placed on the table, and the 'dressing' which we could all dip into, was something I had not experienced as a child growing up in Old Canning Town. Food there then was a basic necessity. 'Eat up and shut up', was the order of the day. Sister Marie did not eat her greens one day and she was not allowed to leave the table until she did, which took quite a while. Apart from the greens, we ate what was placed before us and that was it.

Another experience for me in Lille was a mussel bar. Again, we sat round communal tables, each with a copious supply of mussels, which had been cooked in white wine and garlic. Freshly cooked bread was freely available. There was a large bowl in the centre of the table into which we threw the empty shells. It was a pleasant occasion, friendly banter, beer and coffee, and the 'ping, ping' of shells as they were thrown into the bowl. One man bought Peggy and me a cherry brandy but another pinched my bottom as I left, to which I objected, but Marcel said, 'Oh, c'est la vie.'

By now, we had become quite enchanted with France and whilst we were looking round Lille, we went into a music shop and bought some sheet music. Edith Piaff was popular then, and I bought 'La Vie en Rose', 'Au Chile', and 'La Belle au Bois Dormant', and tried to play these, on the piano, when I returned home.

As August drew to a close, we thought it was time to return. I had still not received my exam result. We were out of money and Peggy had frequent pains in her chest. So on the 2nd September we took a train from Lille to Dieppe, from where we made the crossing for home. When I arrived home, I was pleased to discover that I had passed 'Inter'. I now had to confirm that I had a place at Southampton University. Actually, then it was Southampton University College, a part of London University. It received University status in 1951.

We'd had a wonderful time in France and met many interesting people. No disasters had occurred and we had been overwhelmed with kindness. We had been wined, dined, flattered and courted. For a while I received letters from Reg, Johnny, Gerard, Jean and Andrée, the Tunisian. Peter 'phoned several times, but I was always out. The correspondence petered out when I failed to reply.

It was the last time that Peggy was to undertake such an adventurous holiday. The pains in her chest had been more serious than either of us had realized. I should have been more discerning, but we were both so

Return from France. Walking along Oxford St., after listening to Tony Turner at Lincoln's Inn. Pat, me, Eddie, Peggy. 7th September 1948

convinced of our invulnerability that we could not contemplate that Peggy had other than a cold. For the first three months on her return she continued to feel unwell, and she eventually saw a doctor. First a swollen gland on a bronchial tube was diagnosed and then tuberculosis. This was quite a blow, especially as Peggy had suffered from diabetes since she was seventeen. Throughout her travels in France she had been injecting herself with insulin twice a day. She had become skilled in adjusting the insulin dose to her food intake and thought she had coped very well. Fortunately, streptomycin was now being successfully used in the treatment of TB and after a course of treatment she was fit again. I went to stay with her in Martham, at the end of my first year at Southampton University, during the summer break. That was the first time we had been together since the French holiday. Her mother kept a very strict regime and Peggy was allowed up for just four hours a day. She was, however, feeling very fit, and one day, when her mother was shopping in Norwich, Peggy 'phoned for a taxi, and flew the nest. Poor Mrs. Temple. She had been so supportive, but Peggy had found the restrictions intolerable. She went first to lodgings and then she and Ted Wilmot found furnished accommodation together. They eventually were able to rent a Crown property in Hackney, facing Victoria Park, and 'lived happily ever after'. I was always most welcome there and could stay whenever I liked.

At first, when I returned from France, I went to live with my mother in Seldson Road. Now, after an exciting time in France, I had to get down to the serious business of living. There was still a few weeks to go before I could go to Southampton, where I would then begin to exist on the FETS grant. I was fortunate enough to find a job at the Provincial Insurance Office in Ilford as a typist, which kept the wolf from the door for a few weeks.

What a different world I was about to enter, and how fortunate I was. I had come through a 'hit and miss' primary education and just by the skin of my teeth escaped a secondary education with a school leaving age of fourteen. After three years at the Russell School, the Second World War had commenced and I was evacuated. Fortunately I was not traumatised by this event as I might have been had I been younger. I had cycled through an area of time-bombs during the first day of the Blitz, with Rene; an incendiary bomb had burned a hole in my bed and a house had collapsed around me. Had I been a male, I might have made the ultimate sacrifice like my uncle, my half brother and my cousin. I had learned a great deal at the TB Clinic and been inspired to try to seek solutions to the problems of poverty and war. Through my membership of the Russell Old Students' Association and the good friends I had made there, I had been introduced to music, the theatre and many other cultural pursuits. Although my income had never been much more than enough to carry me through to the following week, I had been to Devon, Dorset, the Peak District, the Lake District, The Pennines, Wales and Ireland and discovered breathtaking landscapes, of which as a child I had been completely unaware. I had also seen some of the devastating effects of war during my visits to Mons and France.

I was fortunate in that more opportunities were available to me than there had been a few generations previously. My mother was born at the beginning of the century, and as I stood poised to enter university, I reflected on what a different world it was fifty years ago. When I told my mother I was to go to Southampton University, she said, 'Southampton? That's funny. I was married there.' And so she was. It was only twenty-eight years previously and yet how different our lives were. She had never discovered the beauties of the Lake District, which I know she would have loved. In fact, to my knowledge, apart from being married in Southampton, and visiting Pat and Eddie in Devon, she had never been further than London and the Home Counties. My father, in trying to escape his environment had become a boxer and suffered brain damage, and he wasn't a happy man. There were so many questions to be answered and problems to be solved.

The sun was shining when I arrived in Southampton. I enquired the way to Shirley where I was to lodge. As I walked up the hill, out of the station, I was full of excitement and ready to face the challenge. This certainly was another world, another life.

– 11 –

Epilogue

That was fifty years ago. And what was to happen next? I'm afraid that is another story, several stories in fact, the stories my brothers and sisters could tell. I'll leave that to them. We broke up as a family in 1939 when five of us were evacuated. We could not be further apart now. Apart from me, only Lawrie remains in this country. His 'dynasty' in Essex grows larger every year. Marie and Eddie are in New Zealand, Jimmy is in Thailand and Patricia is in Canada. Their children and grandchildren have roots in countries far removed from England. What do they know of Old Canning Town or of West Ham? What do they care? Old Canning Town no longer exists, at least not as a place where a tight-knit community lived and died. All the more reason for putting on record the fact that such a place did exist and for portraying some of the conditions and events that had an impact on those of us who lived in that almost forgotten part of London's East End.

Part of Wharf Street, where I lived, has survived, and also the two 'main' roads, Stephenson Street and Bidder Street, but these now exist just to serve a scattering of ware-houses, small industries and businesses. Previously they were lined with densely packed, Victorian, terraced houses and enclosed within them a maze of tiny streets and alley-ways. The Durham Arms is still there, but it doesn't seem to cater now for courting couples or for those requiring just a 'take-away' jug of ale, nor for the local lads and dads, who on their annual day out threw their pennies to eager children as the 'charabanc' pulled away. It recently figured in a CID covert operation called 'Fantasy', largely targeting organized criminals in London's East End. In a report in the *Guardian* newspaper, on March 4th, 2000, the Durham Arms was described as a 'notorious villains pub, where guns were marketed and international drug deals worked out'. It was secretly purchased by the Met. when it came on the market. The pub was staffed by two under-cover officers and hidden microphones were placed on the tables and bar and a camera fitted in the dart board. However, during the investigations, 'a corrupt link between the police and south-east London drug traffickers surfaced.' I wonder what they thought of my husband and me, when we dropped in, asking questions, on our trip to Wharf Street. We thought the barman/landlord looked at us rather strangely when we asked him how long he had been there. Drug trafficking? We don't even smoke cigarettes.

teen. After three years at the Russell School, the Second World War had commenced and I was evacuated. Fortunately I was not traumatised by this event as I might have been had I been younger. I had cycled through an area of time-bombs during the first day of the Blitz, with Rene; an incendiary bomb had burned a hole in my bed and a house had collapsed around me. Had I been a male, I might have made the ultimate sacrifice like my uncle, my half brother and my cousin. I had learned a great deal at the TB Clinic and been inspired to try to seek solutions to the problems of poverty and war. Through my membership of the Russell Old Students' Association and the good friends I had made there, I had been introduced to music, the theatre and many other cultural pursuits. Although my income had never been much more than enough to carry me through to the following week, I had been to Devon, Dorset, the Peak District, the Lake District, The Pennines, Wales and Ireland and discovered breathtaking landscapes, of which as a child I had been completely unaware. I had also seen some of the devastating effects of war during my visits to Mons and France.

I was fortunate in that more opportunities were available to me than there had been a few generations previously. My mother was born at the beginning of the century, and as I stood poised to enter university, I reflected on what a different world it was fifty years ago. When I told my mother I was to go to Southampton University, she said, 'Southampton? That's funny. I was married there.' And so she was. It was only twenty-eight years previously and yet how different our lives were. She had never discovered the beauties of the Lake District, which I know she would have loved. In fact, to my knowledge, apart from being married in Southampton, and visiting Pat and Eddie in Devon, she had never been further than London and the Home Counties. My father, in trying to escape his environment had become a boxer and suffered brain damage, and he wasn't a happy man. There were so many questions to be answered and problems to be solved.

The sun was shining when I arrived in Southampton. I enquired the way to Shirley where I was to lodge. As I walked up the hill, out of the station, I was full of excitement and ready to face the challenge. This certainly was another world, another life.

– 11 –

Epilogue

That was fifty years ago. And what was to happen next? I'm afraid that is another story, several stories in fact, the stories my brothers and sisters could tell. I'll leave that to them. We broke up as a family in 1939 when five of us were evacuated. We could not be further apart now. Apart from me, only Lawrie remains in this country. His 'dynasty' in Essex grows larger every year. Marie and Eddie are in New Zealand, Jimmy is in Thailand and Patricia is in Canada. Their children and grandchildren have roots in countries far removed from England. What do they know of Old Canning Town or of West Ham? What do they care? Old Canning Town no longer exists, at least not as a place where a tight-knit community lived and died. All the more reason for putting on record the fact that such a place did exist and for portraying some of the conditions and events that had an impact on those of us who lived in that almost forgotten part of London's East End.

Part of Wharf Street, where I lived, has survived, and also the two 'main' roads, Stephenson Street and Bidder Street, but these now exist just to serve a scattering of ware-houses, small industries and businesses. Previously they were lined with densely packed, Victorian, terraced houses and enclosed within them a maze of tiny streets and alley-ways. The Durham Arms is still there, but it doesn't seem to cater now for courting couples or for those requiring just a 'take-away' jug of ale, nor for the local lads and dads, who on their annual day out threw their pennies to eager children as the 'charabanc' pulled away. It recently figured in a CID covert operation called 'Fantasy', largely targeting organized criminals in London's East End. In a report in the *Guardian* newspaper, on March 4th, 2000, the Durham Arms was described as a 'notorious villains pub, where guns were marketed and international drug deals worked out'. It was secretly purchased by the Met. when it came on the market. The pub was staffed by two under-cover officers and hidden microphones were placed on the tables and bar and a camera fitted in the dart board. However, during the investigations, 'a corrupt link between the police and south-east London drug traffickers surfaced.' I wonder what they thought of my husband and me, when we dropped in, asking questions, on our trip to Wharf Street. We thought the barman/landlord looked at us rather strangely when we asked him how long he had been there. Drug trafficking? We don't even smoke cigarettes.

EPILOGUE

So it seems the reputation of Old Canning Town lives on. Its notoriety has come full circle, but it is now in a different league. Gone are the days of 'footpads' and fisticuffs. It is now guns, drugs, and 'corruption in the Met'. If Marie and I could be looking out of our bedroom window in Wharf Street, now, who knows what we might discover?

The area, now, is no longer the backwater it once was. The old Canning Town LNER station has been demolished. A magnificent new station has been built, just opposite, on the south side of Barking Road. It occupies part of Victoria Dock Road, once frequented by Lascars, and where once stood rows of impoverished Victorian dwellings. It serves the Docklands Light Railway, and the Jubilee line. When I alighted from the station, recently, I was completely disoriented, being unaware of its new location and that the old station no longer existed. I was directed to the Bridge House Tavern, which I reached after risking life and limb to cross the post-war Newham Way. When I saw the street sign Bidder Street, I knew I was on 'home' ground.

Any visitor travelling from a distance, in the quest perhaps for family history, would find no difficulty now in reaching Canning Town. On the Jubilee line, it is just twenty minutes from Waterloo, and just five minutes from Greenwich North and the much publicised Dome, which incidentally is clearly visible from the Iron Bridge.

How different life was in 1948, when I travelled hopefully to Southampton. I entered into university life with enthusiasm and optimism. There were so many different societies and clubs to join. I joined the Socialist Society and soon became its secretary. I played for the netball team and was awarded my colours. In the first week I was invited to take part in the 'freshers' debate. The subject was, 'This house would be prepared to fight for King and Country'. Ken Dibben, of the Conservative Society, and a member of the family which owned the local building supplies company, spoke in favour and I opposed the motion, taking up an anti-war position. I was no Rosa Luxemburg, or even Barbara Castle, and I think Ken Dibben won. The Dibben business has greatly expanded since those days.

I had more success in the show *Gaslight Gaieties* which the Dramatic Society put on the following February. It was performed on Southampton pier. As well as being a 'Gaiety Girl' and dancing the 'Can-Can', I was also one of Sweeney Todd's unfortunate clients. We had permission to cut a hole in the stage, over which Sweeney Todd's chair was placed. When he pulled a lever, I disappeared through the hole and landed under the stage on to a pile of straw. He rubbed his hands with glee and said, 'What a lovely tart she'll make!'

But enough of soft landings. I did in fact work very hard. Post-war

Netball team, University College, Southampton, 1949-50 (writer: centre front)

Southampton University was an exciting place to be, with so many ex-service and mature students raising the level of discussion. Their experience of the war years enabled them to bring to discussions a depth of feeling and understanding which is lacking in most school-leavers. Lecturers have since remarked that it was never to be such a stimulating place again. My three closest friends during the first year all did very well. One became a Catering Manager at the Albert Hall, one was a Senior Executive on the board of Marks and Spencer, and Seymour Broadbridge, whom I had known at the South East Essex Technical College, became a University Professor. We remained close friends until he died recently.

In my first year I had the audacity to give a talk to the Jewish Society on the 'Jewish Problem'. Seymour came along together with his friend, John Alexander, from the Connaught Hall of Residence. John was reading History and had served in the Royal Signals during the war. He was not demobbed until 1947, having served in Europe and India and he came to Southampton in 1949. He said he fell in love with me at that meeting because of my audacity, and thought that if he ever had to 'man the barricades', he would like to have me by his side. How could I refuse? I graduated in 1951 and we married a few weeks later. We hope to celebrate our golden wedding soon. We've been on several marches together since, but have manned no barricades.

EPILOGUE

Gaslight Gaieties – the can-can dancers (writer: second from left)

(writer: top row, fourth from left)

My mother emigrated to New Zealand in the spring of 1952 and John and I waved her off from Tilbury. That was the last I saw of her. She died in New Zealand in 1978. When my sister Marie was sorting out her property, she came across the sampler I had made when I was twelve years old, in my first year at the Russell School. I didn't even know that my mother had it. It had survived the blitz, four changes of address, and had been half way round the world. She also had a letter I had sent her describing my first son. Imagine my surprise and pleasure when these arrived by post. The sampler is now framed and hanging in a bedroom. She gave no indication that these meant so much to her. She was a complex character. I looked after Eddie for six months in Southampton when my mother first went to New Zealand, until she could raise the money to send for him. He was then sixteen years old, an intelligent but unhappy 'loner', and he would much rather have stayed. Harry, who had accompanied him on the journey, travelled half way round the world to be with my mother, only for them to separate two years later.

When my mother died, she left her home to Eddie, who was unmarried. He gave away the contents, including all the furniture and sold the delightful detached house below its market value and bought a flat. He lives a very spartan, lonely existence. Marie has been very supportive, when she is allowed to be, but he does not seek the company of others. When John and I went to New Zealand a few years ago, it was our first visit, and the first time I had seen him since he left at sixteen years of age. The only property he had retained was a penknife he said I had bought for him on my first holiday to France with Peggy. We had many intelligent discussions with him and he was pleased to take us on a tour of the Arts Centre in Christchurch. He is one who never reached his potential. I do wonder what he would have been like had he not had such a traumatic break from his family at the age of three. I do worry about Eddie, but there is nothing I can do. Marie does what she can.

I had no further contact with my father after my mother and I left him during the war. At sixty-five, he went into an old people's home, but aggressive outbursts there led eventually to his removal to a psychiatric hospital. In 1973, I was reading the Sunday Times when I came across an article about research that had been carried out on fifteen boxers' brains. This had been carried out by Dr. Corsellis from the Department of Neuropathology at Runwell Hospital, Wickford, in Essex. The case histories of some of the fifteen boxers were outlined, and one of them read remarkably like my father's. I wrote to Dr. Corsellis and he confirmed that my father's brain had indeed been one of the fifteen used in the research. He eventually sent me a copy of the report, which showed that my father had, in fact, suffered brain damage. The report stated that 'There was conclusive evidence that lasting cerebral damage can be incurred from repeated blows to the head. This could lead to loss of memory, speech disturbance, lack of balance, outbursts of violence and eventual dementia.' Boxers suffering from these symptoms were usually just described as 'punchy', a far less sympathetic description than 'a victim of brain damage'. All the brains showed degeneration and loss of nerve cells, not found to the same extent in non-boxers' brains. In twelve cases the septum had been torn.

The newspaper article remarked, 'The case histories in the report .... shed a grim new light on the days when success in the ring could mean the difference between rags and riches but when few men were aware of the misery underlying the glamour.' I can now understand my father's frustration at not being able to express himself in an articulate manner, and resorting to violence and abusive language instead, but I can also appreciate that it wasn't easy for my mother, or anybody else who got in his way. My father died aged eighty-three at the Runwell Hospital.

Sadly I have been to several funerals of close friends in the last twenty years. Ted Wilmot died before Peggy, and she never really came to terms with it. In his later years he had been an education organizer in the Labour Party and was a founder member of the Socialist Environmental and Resources Association, SERA. Right to the last he was writing articles and having discussions on political philosophy. Peggy organized his funeral and it was just as he would have wished. It was a non-religious ceremony. His favourite music was played and there were appropriate readings from Shakespeare and happy reminiscences. Many old friends and socialists gathered in Hackney Town Hall after the funeral, all remembering the days of out-door meetings and public debates, in which Ted was so much involved. As many people remarked, 'Ted would have loved it. He should have been here.' He was never to see the fall of the Berlin wall, or the break up of the Soviet Union, or Yugoslavia, which seemed so impregnable when he was alive. It would not have changed his philosophy, as, like many socialists, he always held the view that the USSR was not a socialist state.

He was not to know of the release of Nelson Mandela either and the dismantling of the apartheid regime in South Africa. Neither was Peggy. She died in 1990 of a heart and lung condition, complicated by fifty years of suffering from diabetes. She had to inject herself twice a day for all that time. It is a pity they were not to experience the elation so many of us felt when Mandela's government came to power.

When Peggy became ill, she left a 'living will', which she placed with the hospital responsible for her care. This stated that she had no wish to be kept alive by mechanical means. She did not wish to be bed-ridden and a burden to others, and she could no longer do the things which gave her pleasure. I was present when she discussed this, quite calmly and logically, with the sister in charge of the intensive care unit at the hospital. I said, 'She has not reached that stage yet!' But I was wrong. Shortly after, various tubes were withdrawn, and she slipped into a coma and died of kidney failure.

Peggy had a 'good' funeral. But then, she organized it herself. My three children and two grandchildren were there, and my two sons organized the music and taped the very many tributes paid to Peggy. One of these was from our friend, and author of *Jack London*, Robert Barltrop. He recalled the time when he first knew us, and were known as 'Peggy and Ivy'. We left the service to the sound of Edith Piaff singing, 'Je ne regrette rien.' I spoke at the reception afterwards and reminisced about the happy days at 'Fagin's Kitchen'.

There is a plaque and a magnolia tree in memory of Peggy in Victoria Park, Hackney. When there was the threat of a major road going through that beautiful park, the Victoria Park Society was formed and Peggy was a founder member and its Secretary. The plaque and tree are in recognition of the work she did for the Society. I was invited to the memorial planting and John and I have been to the Park on several occasions since to see if the tree is in good shape. It is very slow growing. When West Ham ceased to be a borough in 1963, Peggy was given an award 'to place on record their very high appreciation of the valuable services rendered for twenty years.' I now have that framed certificate. She continued to teach for the new Authority, Newham, for another nineteen years and then became Chairman of Governors at a local primary school. Both Peggy and Ted were very much part of the lives of our family. They didn't have any children of their own. They were a sad loss.

I have been to some happy events, too, such as Rene and Jack's golden wedding anniversary, in 1998. Rene organized a family reunion at the same time and as the youngest child of a family of eleven children, that was quite an undertaking. There were nearly a hundred family members present and Rene had drawn up a family tree which was pinned up on the wall of the hotel in Cornwall where the reception was held.

Ferdy and Vera married in 1949, a year after I went to Southampton University and John and I also went to their golden wedding anniversary. Vera, Rene and I were in the same class when we first went to the Russell School.

John and I expect to reach our 'golden' as well, but I do not anticipate a family reunion like Rene's. We'd like to go on a walking exploration somewhere, possibly South Africa, South America or New Zealand. We've been retired for many years now and since doing so have walked in many different countries, including France, Italy, Spain, Morocco, Tunisia, South Africa, Zimbabwe, New Zealand and Cuba. We lead a very busy life and are both active members of the Ramblers Association. After graduation I continued to teach and to raise a family. My teaching experience was divided equally between secondary and primary schools, serving as Careers Mistress for a time, and then Infant Maths Co-ordinator, and Teachers' Centre Organizer. John was a History teacher for many years and then after obtaining a further degree he became a Lecturer in History at a College of Education.

What has given us the greatest happiness and satisfaction, however, has been our three children. We hope we have provided them with a secure, but challenging and loving environment, in which they have been able to develop their potential. All three graduated with good honours degrees. One son is an historian and Doctor of Philosophy, and another is a social researcher and teacher. Our only daughter, Clare, is an imaginative sculptor and Head of Expressive Arts at a school in Dorset. I could expand on their qualities and achievements, but they would not wish me to do so. What we are pleased about is that whilst all three have developed their own interests and concerns, they have nevertheless been mindful of the inequalities and injustices of the world around them. They each have a strong social conscience, which is paramount. This is reflected in their chosen careers. They were fortunate in that during their formative years, a university education was within their reach. There were no tuition fees and subsistence grants were available.

One thing that has concerned me about the past has been the restriction of people's development. Men and women became unskilled labourers, working long hours doing unexciting and repetitive jobs, which left them at the end of the day with very little energy to think of anything else. Their poor education and lack of skills left them with very few options. At least with a wider education, one has the possibility of making a choice. Before the Second World War, there was very little opportunity for children of unskilled workers to enter university and even less opportunity for those of the unemployed and unemployable. The situation improved a little in the fifties and sixties, but today, the percentage from this social class entering university is still too low and present legislation gives us no cause for optimism. So much wasted potential and suppression of talent! I was, indeed, very fortunate that I was able to break the mould, albeit with some help and encouragement, and a bit of luck and determination.

'Men at some time are masters of their fate', said Cassius. 'Their fault, dear Brutus, lies not in our stars, but ourselves.' If only that were so. Perhaps for Cassius and Brutus, but, unfortunately, for many people, circumstances are too oppressive to fight against. And yet, Omar Khayyam's philosophy leaves no room for optimism or endeavour.

> Tis all a chequer-board of nights and days,
> Where destiny with men for pieces plays:
> Hither and thither moves, and mates, and slays,
> And one by one back in the closet lays.

This is too fatalist a philosophy. During the many discussions we had at Fagin's, well into the night, and usually after an outdoor meeting, I came across another philosophy:

> Men make their own history, but they do not make it as they please; they do not make it under circumstances chosen by themselves, but under circumstances directly encountered, given, and transmitted from the past.

This Marxist analysis is closer to my own experience. We can, and do, make choices, but the range of choices is determined by the society into which we are born, and the circumstances in which we find ourselves. I think, regretfully, of the many generations past, who had an extremely limited choice and were unable to realize their aspirations, and hope that future generations will be more nearly masters of their fate.

Now, as we enter a new millennium, one son is in South Africa and another is in South America. My granddaughter has just entered university and her sister is at a Sixth Form College. Like their mother, Clare, both are artistic and practical, and I see in them some of the finer attributes my mother possessed. It is now a hundred years since she was born in 1901. Unfortunately, like many others, for a variety of reasons, she was frustrated in her failure to reach her potential. I do hope that my grandchildren make something more of their lives.

Appendix

Eric's account of 7th September, 1940

WAR-TIME MEMORIES, by Eric Green

Saturday the 7th September started as a glorious autumn day, and to the best of my recollection my morning was as usual, local deliveries to factories, and to ships in the Royal Docks, East London, as a driver for Greengate & Irwell Rubber Co. of Canning Town, London, E.16. I had no idea when I finished work about 12.30 pm that just six hours later East London was to look so different, and our world would be turned upside down. Up to then the war had been an inconvenience, but not much more. A few months earlier, in May, I started my first driving job, and at 17 years old, life was wonderful. Once in my little 10 cwt van, all I saw and thought about was that road in front of me. I had at last begun to live. I just loved driving. When I came home, someone said, 'Rene,' (my younger sister) 'and her friend Ivy Hicks, have gone off on their bikes to Epping Forest for the day'. Nothing unusual in that. In those days our bikes were our main means of transport and pleasure. The roads were so much quieter than these days. Cars were very few and far between, and lorries and vans travelled at about 25 to 30 mph; in fact the bigger lorries were very often slower than we were on our bikes. Cycling was pretty safe and enjoyable.

About 2.30 pm the air-raid sirens began to wail. We didn't take too much notice at first. Lone reconnaissance German planes often set off the air-raid alarm, but after 10 minutes or so the ack-ack guns began to fire and when we heard the big 4.5 guns on Wanstead Flats open up, we knew something different was up. Then we saw the big formations of German bombers coming over, and before the first bombs fell in our vicinity, we were in our Anderson shelters at the bottom of the garden. Being a big family, we had two shelters, facing each other, with a sandbagged dugout entrance between them. Then, as the bombs began to whistle down, some with a dreadful screaming sound, there was a bang in the entrance. We thought a bomb or something had fallen in the entrance, but to our relief it was Rover, our scruffy sheepdog, crashing in at full speed. Poor thing! He was terrified.

We crouched in our shelters, pretty frightened I can tell you, with our first experience of the terrors of war at first hand. This went on for about three hours, the whistling of bombs falling and the ground shaking from the explosions. We all thought it was our lot. We thought nobody could survive this. Then, as things began to quieten down, my father and I climbed out of the shelters, and to our relief, we saw our house was still standing. We had expected everything to be flattened, but when we looked to the end of our row of houses, the last couple were not there. They had been blown up. Then on our right, where there were blocks of flats, four stories high, sticking out of the roofs, were big pieces of metal about 20 feet long. My father said that they were pieces of railway line. We lived opposite the main railway line into the Royal Docks. We then went into the house. The front and back door had been blown off and a lot of glass from the windows was strewn everywhere. My father said, 'I'll check upstairs'. I went out of the front door, or at least where the front door should have been. The first thing I noticed was that the signal box opposite our house was tilted at an angle of 45 degrees and debris was everywhere. Looking back at our house, between our front door and the front door of the house next door, I saw this big hole about five feet across and about four feet deep. Jumping down into it, I could see some metal sticking up. Then my father came out of the house and seeing me down the hole, all excited, took one look and grabbed me by the collar and hauled me out. 'Quick!' he shouted. 'Get everyone back into the shelters. It's an unexploded bomb!' Whilst I went out the back shouting, 'Get back into the shelters! There's an unexploded bomb in front of the house,' my father ran up the road to warn the air-raid wardens. The metal I could see in the hole must have been the top of the tail fins of the bomb and I had jumped down on top of it. The all clear had now sounded and people thought they were now safe, but it was not over yet. Every now and again unexploded bombs were going off. We were now being told to get out of the shelters and go to the school, which was at the back of our house.

My mother was in a terrible state, what with the bombs and being told that our neighbours, a few doors away, had received a direct hit on their shelter and that their bodies were found on the railway line opposite. She now realized my sister Rene and her friend were out there somewhere, but just as we were being told to go to the school, they turned up, very frightened and in tears. Ivy Hicks, my sister's friend, said, 'I must go home. My mum will be in a right state.' I volunteered to see her home. She only lived about half a mile away. 'I wont be long,' I said to my Mum and Dad and I got my bike out of the shed, which was still standing, and my tin hat, (I was a messenger boy for the London Fire Brigade) and said, 'Come on, Ivy. Let's go'. We made the first 50 yards in a straight line towards her home, over bricks, rubble and God knows what and then our first diversion. 'You can't go up the hill and over the railway line, laddie. There are fifty or more unexploded bombs all the way along the railway line,' said the air-raid warden. So off we went to the left, down past Gainsborough Road school, where my family were, up Grange Road, going in the complete opposite direction to the way we wanted to go. I knew a little alleyway and we dodged the air-raid wardens and came out into Hermit Road, and then into the main Barking Road. Here, everywhere was in chaos, shop windows all blown in, bricks and debris covering the road, and footpaths were non existent. We had to walk in the road most of the time and we had to pick our bikes up on to our shoulders and climb over the rubble. Then just before Canning Town Station, we saw a double-decker bus down a bomb hole. Just about then I remember a warden shouting, 'This is no time to be out with your girl friend on bikes'. By this time we were becoming immune to air-raid wardens telling us we couldn't use this road or that road because of unexploded bombs and were ignoring them. Ivy was desperate to get home to see if her family were all right, so we passed Canning Town Station into Stephenson Street, then turned into Wharf Street, where Ivy lived. There, coming towards us, were Ivy's mum and her sister. Ivy's mum started having a right go at me for being out with her daughter. At this point, my courage failed me. I jumped on my bike and rode off as fast as the bricks and rubble would allow me. This time, I went the short way, past the unexploded bombs, past the blown up footbridge, past air-raid wardens shouting at me. 'Messenger boy! Urgent message for the fire brigade,' I shouted back, and kept on pedalling, at least where I could.

I got back to the school where my family all were, and then went off again with my dad to try and get something to eat for us all. We did get some sandwiches from a mobile canteen. Not long after getting back, at about 9 pm, 'our time bomb' as we came to call it, blew up, destroying most of our house. I shall never forget the noise, with all the bricks and debris falling on to the school roof. We all thought the school roof was going to collapse on us, but it held firm. We spent that night at the school. Next day we salvaged what we could from our house, clothing, blankets, etc. and with a coster-monger's barrow, trucked it all round to my eldest brother's house, who lived a couple of miles away near the Spotted Dog pub, Forest Gate. We spent that night in his and his next door neighbour's shelters. In the early hours of the morning, a 1,000 lb bomb dropped in the gardens behind us and the crater was within 2 to 3 feet of our shelters. We heard that bomb come down, screaming all the way. I remember thinking to myself, 'We will be all right, as they say you don't hear the bomb that hits you.' That useless bit of information was only out by a couple of feet. We all survived that, completely unhurt, but my brother's house was wrecked and we survived the night at another brother's house, when a landmine came down and was hanging in a tree by its parachute, only about thirty yards away. When we came out of the shelters we walked into a tangle of wires. I thought to myself, 'It's a booby trap,' but it was the land mine, which had pulled down all the phone and radio wires.

Those three days and nights have lived in my mind for nearly sixty years, but that's life. We were a family of thirteen, mum, dad, and eleven children and we all survived the war, in spite of those three days and nights of hell. Except one brother, who sadly was killed just before D-day.

Update

On a recent visit to Old Canning Town, I called in at the Durham Arms. I spoke to the licensee, Mr. T. J. Luggar, and mentioned the article in the *Guardian* of March 4th 2000 (see page 146). He said he was upset about the tone of the article and forwarded a complaint to the editor. An apology was subsequently published on March 30th, which stated that the events described took place before Mr. Luggar took over and reported 'We have no reason to suggest that any of the activities mentioned have continued into Mr. Luggar's tenure.'

I had made this visit with my brother Jimmy to photograph familiar landmarks before they disappeared beneath concrete. Alas, I arrived too late for some. The Bridge House Tavern (page 27) was no more – the site was boarded up and JCBs were very much in evidence. The area was crisscrossed by power lines, and the muddy banks of Bow Creek, close to the station, were also being attacked. I enquired whether the days of the Durham Arms were numbered and I was informed that they were. A compulsory purchase order was a possibility, and the entire area was to be the subject of massive development.

If some space is set aside for residential building, will it be a human-scale neighbourhood development as on the nearby Lansbury estate? And if it is, would I want to live there? I wonder.

POSTSCRIPT - 2002

It has surprised me just how much interest has been generated by the publication of this book. It has had many favourable reviews by local history societies, as well as one in a national daily paper and two in the Newham Recorder. One is pending by the Socialist History Society and another by the Southampton University's School of Education publication, 'Auto/Biography'. Several readers have recommended it to their local library, and a Canadian History Lecturer on the urban working class is also interested. Although it was only made available to the West Ham Bookshop, I am now receiving orders from many other book shops more distant. I have had many appreciative letters and phone calls, some from as far afield as California and Toronto. At a 'signing' at the Newham Bookshop I met a pupil from the first school at which I taught, Ashburton Senior Girls school, in Custom House, and also a pupil, Peter Andrew, from Three Mills School, Stratford. As a result of this very favourable response I have been encouraged to have further copies printed, and I have used the occasion to make a few minor corrections and to add this postscript. It has also given me the opportunity to thank Vivian Archer of the Newham Bookshop for not hesitating to accept and promote my book. The Editor of the Newham Recorder was also supportive, and Roy Hibbard from East Ham, though previously unacquainted with me, has been a driving force in promoting the book. Special thanks are also due to Denis Galvin for his review in *The Cockney Ancestor* and to Eddie Dare for his sensitive and thoughtful reviews for several History Societies.

What has delighted me in particular has been making contact with former neighbours from Old Canning Town. Other readers who had not themselves lived in Old Canning Town remembered stories from their parents and grandparents and thanked me for graphically describing life there. Mrs. K. McDonagh wrote, 'My mother came from Old Canning Town and you are the first person I have heard call it that apart from my mother'. Haydn Williams wrote, 'One of my oldest memories is hearing my grandparents and great aunts and uncles singing, after a few drinks, the last line of a popular song, *It's just a shanty in Old Canning Town.*' George Pray from Kates Cottages in Junction Street, and now living in Toronto, reminds me that once there were nine pubs in Old Canning Town, and lists their names and locations. Only two remain now, the Dartmouth Arms and the Durham Arms, but for how long? The street sign, 'Wharf Street' is attached to the wall of the Durham Arms, and the Licensee, Terry Luggar, hopes to salvage this for me, should the pub be demolished. Mary Long, nee Sullivan, now from California, lived in Bidder Street, and points out that our houses were shattered by the same land-mine. She was only 7 years old at the time and living now in a 'different world' found it difficult to remember all the details. She was enthralled to read my account. It evoked so many memories. After the bombing, Mary's family went to the relative safety of Canvey Island, but her mother returned to Canning Town once a week to clean the front doorstep of their new house in Percy Road.

Harry Marshall, now aged 85 years, was in the early 1930s working as a 'wireman's mate' and helped install electricity in many houses in West Ham, including those in Wharf Street! Little did he know that after he had finished, my father whacked me with his walking stick for switching on the lights. During the course of his work he had access to bedrooms, and discovered that, 'many of the beds were covered by immaculate bedspreads, emblazoned with the words, *Shaw Saville, Houlder Line, Nelson Line, Port Line* and *P&O.*' Harry, being very knowledgeable about boxing, confirmed that Digger Stanley, who my father fought, was world bantam weight champion from 1906 to 1912. He sent me a photo, reputedly the only recorded photo of Digger in existence. Harry, and many other Old Canning Town residents, born before me, and whose connections with the area went back further, passed on to me a great deal of fascinating information.

Daphne Farmer, now of Rhode Island, USA, is desperate for a photo of St. Gabriel's Church, which was off Wellington Street. She writes, 'All my grandparents and great-grandparents lived in Old Canning Town, and several of the offspring were baptised in St. Gabriel's. I would dearly like a photo. Twenty two archives or people have been contacted, to no avail'. Sadly, the church was destroyed during the blitz.

In the epilogue to my book, I wrote that I was fortunate to have 'broken the mould'. From my correspondence, it seems that there were many others who did so, too. In spite of leaving school at 16, or even 14, many achieved academic success by availing themselves of the opportunities offered by West Ham. There were, for instance, 'Continuation Schools', such as the Shakespeare and Lister Institutes. As Harry Marshall wrote, 'Those schools were the fore-runners of today's C.F.E.s. West Ham education committee should be proud of that pioneering introduction'.

But what of the opportunities for youngsters today? Although, during the last fifty years, the proportion of students entering university has increased enormously, according to the UCCA Statistical Supplement, admissions from children from unskilled working class parents remains abysmally low. Children from my 'socio-economic' group would fare much the same today as we did sixty years ago. Even Peter Mandelson, a former Labour cabinet Minister, writing in *The Guardian* on 17/5/2002, states that ....'Labour has talked a good game about greater social mobility, including obligatory denunciations of snobbery, racial prejudice, the closed shops of the professions and the restricted access to universities and the civil service. But has it really taken these citadels by storm and made a difference for the sort of young people who live in my constituency and feel shut out because so many paths are barred to them? The answer is no. We just tinkered. Britain remains a society with too many elites and scarred by poverty of aspirations among the less affluent.' I find this very sad. But what can we do? I sometimes wish there was the same drive to overcome the injustices in society as was evident when I was a 'maid in West Ham.'

POSTSCRIPT - 2004

As a self-publisher I was rather conservative in estimating the number of books I should have had printed, but as 'Maid in West Ham' is now available in several bookshops, demand has continued. A further print run has therefore been necessary. Some readers first came across the book in their local library and I have had many letters from those who have obtained the book this way.

I was delighted to receive six, single-spaced, typed A4 pages from a 93 year old former Customs Officer from Harwich who obtained a copy from his local library. He worked in the London Docks from 1932 to 1938 and came to know West Ham when he was posted to the Albert Dock. He said that although autobiographical accounts 'were not his scene', he was attracted by the title, and found the book so evocative that he was moved to share some of his unique and valuable experience with me. He writes, 'You would have shared my horror at seeing a fleet of dustcarts proceeding through West Ham loaded with perfectly good bananas bound for destruction because they were ripe, and passing so much poverty where they would have been good and tasteful nourishment. Even worse, any ripe fruit was deposited in bins at the quayside for collection and dockers were actually prosecuted for helping themselves to these'. He recalled a wealth of memories and generously said it was my book that had rekindled them.

My erstwhile dock-worker neighbour would have been amused to know that I was in friendly correspondence with a former Customs Officer, but also happy to know that my book is now on the shelves in the Museum at Docklands Shop at West India Quay, not too far from Wharf Street. No more unloading of sugar and spice for George, however. Sadly, he, like many other dockers, did not live to see the transformation of the Docks, where they waited, hopefully, 'on the stones' to be selected for low-paid and often unpleasant work. He would not recognise the Victoria Dock or any of the Docks where he once worked. Many, like the St. Katharine Dock, are now tourist attractions.

Growing up in West Ham, I had assumed it would last forever and that we were 'all of a kind'. It was thus, and always would be. From the many letters I have received I now realize that West Ham was created by people from a variety of backgrounds. There were displaced illiterate farm labourers, immigrants, impoverished job-seekers, some who had seen better times but also some 'who had made it', and all with varying aspirations, but united by the need to earn a living. Subsequent generations have moved on, with an improved standard of living bearing no resemblance to that of their forebears. West Ham still attracts a diverse population from an even greater range of cultures but still with the unifying desire to find work and raise families. They, too, will move on, as we did.

Not everyone, however, has had, or will have, the good fortune to take their 'street' with them. On a recent visit to the District Six Museum in Cape Town, I learnt that, after the streets there were bull-dozed in 1966, in the name of apartheid, the street signs were secretly salvaged and hidden in a cellar. I began to wonder what had happened to all the street signs of West Ham which had become obsolete when there were no streets in which to hang them and was determined that WHARF STREET, E.16 would not finish up in the scrapyard. I am now delighted to report that, since writing 'Postscript - 2002', I have received, through the post but not through my letter-box, a long, rigid parcel, measuring 4 feet by 9 inches, and covered by nineteen postage stamps. It was the WHARF STREET E.16 name plate, which became redundant when the Durham Arms underwent a face-lift. Terry Luggar, the Licensee, had kept his word. When I telephoned my brother Jimmy in Thailand, he became emotional. 'Isn't it fantastic!' he said. 'It is like coming home'; though why he should want to do so beggars belief.

WHARF STREET E.16 now hangs proudly on my house wall in Winchester and will eventually be framed by a variegated ivy. It pleases me that a street sign from one of the most deprived areas of England should be placed on the wall of a house in one of the most affluent. Don't ask me why I should care. It's a mystery to me, too.

POSTSCRIPT - 2010

It is six years since my last postscript and my stock of 'Maid in West Ham' is now very low. I had thought that, as I am now in my ninth decade, I would 'call it a day'. However, I have been encouraged to go for another reprint as there has been a resurgence of interest in my book. This may be in part because there has also been an increasing interest in West Ham. In 2005, London won the bid to host the 2012 Olympic Games. A suitable site had to be found where land values were not high and where the local people were not in a position to raise too much objection to their relocation.

An area, criss-crossed by a tangle of thirteen constantly shifting waterways, known as the Bow back rivers and flowing into Bow Creek, was selected. The waterways have suffered from centuries of neglect and the land was used for polluting industries and landfill. This was the unfortunate legacy of the great King Alfred, who dammed the river Lea to prevent the approaching Viking longships, further up river, from reaching the Thames. The River Lea then spilled over, forming a network of channels. As well as dangerous chemicals and radio-active materials, many bombs, courtesy of the Luftwaffe, were embedded in the mud. Notwithstanding this, millions of people lived, worked and died in the vicinity. Bow Creek was in fact at the end of Wharf Street and bordered Old Canning Town. Thanks to the siting of the Olympic Games, billions of pounds have now been spent on cleaning and decontaminating the area. Sadly it has come too late for many. Old Canning Town no longer exists as a community of people but its memory is still strong in the minds of those who once lived there.

Another road on the border of Bow Creek was Shipwright Street. A former Wharf Street neighbour, Jessie Waite, once lived there as a child. As a result of her reading 'Maid in West Ham', she contacted me and kindly sent me this photo of the children who lived nearby, taken in 1922 outside her grandmother's house. Such was the strong sense of community that she could remember nearly every person in the picture.

I quote here from her letter:

"<u>Top Left</u> Mrs Bull, Harry Reed holding his sister, Fanny Pringle holding her youngest sister Nellie, Wag, girl Evans holding unknown baby, Ada Morris holding one of the Grays, girl Ellis, Sammy Kelly next to Wag.
<u>2nd Line</u> Our Fred, Nora Smith, girl Webster, one of the Peppers, Maudie Sharp, another Driscoll, boy Evans, miss one, Rosie Webster, Lily Eaton (end of line).
<u>3rd Row</u> 5th one in Dolly Sharp, another Webster, Rosie Reed (killed in raid), another Reed, Violet Evans, Higgins, Webster.
That's me in front of Fred, 4th one in front row, Louie Barwick, Tommy Dedman, 7th along Daisy Clark, front row, Johnnie Bassenger killed in war."

It would be great if any readers recognised family members, or even themselves, in this photo. One picture in my book which evoked memories was that of the Brown family on page 30. Marie Rose Higgs was surprised to see a picture of her mother, Lizzie Brown. She was delighted to have made contact with the family that had figured so large in the conversations of the three Brown sisters. I last saw Marie's mother on the morning after the night raid of 19th March, 1941, when we sat amongst the rubble of our homes. Lizzie's father was missing and she thought she saw articles of his clothing on the tall tree at the end of our garden. However, after contacting the Newham registrar recently, it was revealed that Marie's grandfather was discovered in the ruins of his home five days later. The Vicar of St. Mathias Church was also killed that night. He was probably passing by.

Apart from personal photos, there seemed to have been a dearth of photographic evidence of life in Old Canning Town. However, recently, Kathy Taylor as a result of her work for Newham Heritage and Archives, came across some previously unrecorded photos. One was of the allotments close to the Cooperage (see map on page 17) at the northern end of Old Canning Town. It showed happy, tidy and well-behaved children, all carrying gardening tools. This was not my memory of the time when my street mates and I were once reprimanded for playing among the cabbages and unearthing a radish or two. Another picture showed the inside of the much loved Wellington Nursery School, held at the former Duke of Wellington public house. My brother Eddie experienced many happy days there until 1st September, 1939, when the entire nursery school was evacuated to a grand house in Bishops Stortford. The ensuing blitz the following year sadly put an end to the Wellington Nursery School.

One establishment which has survived, in a neighbouring local authority, has been Valentines Mansion in Ilford. I mention it here as it was where my father's father, also named James, was born in 1866. Not being under any illusion that my paternal forebears were members of the aristocracy I was bemused, until Georgina Green, a research historian, enlightened me. Valentines Mansion was once owned by Mrs. Sarah Ingleby, who did much to help the local community, including the Hicks family who lived close by, in Beehive Lane. As my great grandmother already had seven children, it seems likely that she was the fortunate recipient of Mrs. Ingleby's beneficence. After standing empty for many years, the Mansion has now been restored with funds from Redbridge Council and the Heritage Lottery Fund and strong local support.

Unfortunately, the Bancroft Boys Club (pages 91, 92), which was very popular with local boys, did not survive. However, many of their letters written when they were in the services, to Ferdy Waterson, did survive and recently came into my possession. After Ferdy died, his daughter Jane came across bundles of these letters from 25 of the lads and passed them on to me. I then became the custodian of over a hundred letters, written nearly 70 years ago. The Club, sponsored by the Bancroft's School at Woodford Green and formed in 1911, has now closed and the building demolished. As custodian of the letters, I thought them too important to be just bundled up again and hidden in archives. I contacted the Headmaster of the school and suggested the letters were worthy of consideration and documentation. As a result, Jeremy Blomfield, the Deputy Head, called on me and we discussed the matter. He expects to retire shortly and when he does he will read through the letters and mention them in a 'History of the Bancroft Boys Club' which he hopes to write.

Another source for delving into the past has been the Newham History Website. As a former West Ham boxer, my father's name was mentioned. My brother, now in New Zealand, and who bore his name, was contacted by the grandson of Charlotte, my father's first wife. Only in her declining years did Charlotte reveal my father's name. Her memory was not a happy one. I was able to reassure the loving grandson that Charlotte and my mother, having a great deal in common, gave each other support and consolation. I sent him a copy of the photograph, shown on page three. It was the only picture he had seen of his grandmother as a young woman. We exchanged many friendly and interesting emails and the ensuing correspondence revealed that Charlotte and James Hicks were patients in their final years at the Runwell Hospital's Psychiatric Unit, at the same time. What a bizarre coincidence! Charlotte and her grandson did not share a political ideology. He had been a Tory M.P. for thirteen years and lost his seat when the Labour Party was elected in 1997.

Another thirteen years have since passed and a General Election is due shortly, the outcome of which is uncertain. John and I will celebrate our diamond wedding next year and have seen many governments come and go, for better or worse. One major improvement though, has been the establishment of the National Health Service. We are both thankful for and dependant on the service it provides. We are fortunate to have lived healthy and active lives for so long but the downside is that we cannot share it with our many close friends and members of the family who are no longer with us. Sadly, my sister Marie died a few years ago in New Zealand, from emphysema, brought on by cigarette smoking when she was in the WAAF's and then continued for some years afterwards. I do miss her weekly phone calls to me.

On a happier note, our first grandson, the much desired child of Becky and our son John was safely delivered a few months ago, not in a mansion, but in a National Health Service hospital. The care and support that Becky received was second to none, and is widely available. Now, together with loving parents and two sets of supportive grandparents, he has the possibility of a more fulfilling life than many of my forbears experienced. However, inequalities of opportunity in our society still exist, and I hope that by reading my book, he will discover what efforts we made to overcome these, and even gained some satisfaction and pleasure in doing so.